What Readers Are Saying...

"Beautifully expressed God-centered advice on how to navigate singleness in today's world and remember your true identity and worth in Christ. Cherie and Lona cover every topic with non-judgmental honesty, vulnerability, and humor. It's a 'must read' for single ladies of all ages as they wait for MOYD!"
~Karen Keeley, Nashville, TN
Casting Director/Songwriter/Producer, Karenkeeleycasting.com

"I love this book! I am already thinking of people who need to read this book right now! I love the practical application and biblical references that back up all of their advice.
Single ladies of all ages will benefit from these principles.
I will be praying for great success of this book.
Much needed in today's world!"
~Lori Termale, Warwick, RI
Women's Pastor, Legacychurchri.com

"*MEET MOYD* is an empowering message for single ladies. Cherie & Lona help the reader understand God's Word to emphasize the importance of self-worth in Christ and the importance of waiting for the right man that God has predestined for you. It's valuable because it helps women to embrace their identity in Christ and not settle for less in a spouse. Having the interactive exercises after each chapter enhances the learning experience and has helped me apply the concepts to my own life. *MEET MOYD* provides practical tools to grow spiritually while navigating your journey to find the right man! This is a great gift for all those who are single, whether for yourself or a friend."
~Cathy Paliotta, Smithfield, RI
"The Sauce Boss," Cucinadicatherina.com

MEET MOYD

A little book of advice to help you
meet the **M**an **O**f **Y**our **D**reams

Cherie Adams & Lona Renée Fraser

ISBN: 979-8-218-41946-2
Library of Congress Control Number: 2024908242

Notice of Liability
The authors have made every effort to check and ensure the accuracy of the information presented in this book. However, the information herein is sold without warranty, either expressed or implied. Neither the author, publisher, nor any dealer or distributor of this book will be held liable for any damages caused either directly or indirectly by the instructions and information contained in this book.

Book cover design by Cherie Adams.

Cherie Adams photograph taken by Kim Brantley Photography, Copyright ©2024. All rights reserved.
Lona Renée Fraser photograph taken by Karissa Selby, Copyright ©2016. All rights reserved.

Printed in the United States of America.

Dolce Vita Publishing
Franklin, TN

From Cherie

♥

To my Curly Girly—Ellianna Capri, may Jesus be your MOYD all the days of your life.

To Santiago & Sebastiano, may you always keep Jesus close to your heart and become the MOYD your future wives are searching for.

To Kevin "E"- for everything Adams—the MOYD I have always dreamt of.
I am so thankful for the example you set for our children.
I love you with all of my heart!

Most of all, to Jesus for being there through the messy parts, You were my first MOYD and always will be.

♥

From Lona

♥

To my husband Jim, thank you for opening the car door for me.

To my son Brendan and daughter Kayla, I love the way you love and care for others. You are my continual inspiration to show this same kind of affection through my writing.

♥

Contents

Introduction

"Why then the world's mine oyster,
which I with sword will open." - William Shakespeare
(Author of the most famous love story ever told —Romeo & Juliet)

MEET MOYD is a book of advice intended to help you find MOYD—The man of your dreams. Many years ago, I (Cherie) started keeping a list of the "do's & don'ts of dating." I always thought this would make a funny little booklet and that I would release it to the world someday! I went through a few stormy seasons during my single years. Dating to me was like trying to find a buried treasure, and I sifted through the wrong guys for quite some time, worried that I would never find the man of my dreams—MOYD. Thank God I was wrong!

A year ago, I thought it would be fun to ask my friend Lona to join me in developing this idea I had for single ladies called ***MEET MOYD*** and she came on board. We have had many hilarious lunch meetings mixed with some really serious ones. I don't think either one of us realized the tender ache we have in our hearts for single ladies.

Thinking back on those years, while most days were spent having the time of our lives, we cringe at some of the foolish things we did. We've learned a lot from our past mistakes and thank God for our mentors. They are the women who have gone before us whose marriages have withstood the storms of life and tests of time. This book is not a book of rules and regulations (actually...☺...LOL). What began as a funny little book turned into an easy-to-read, compassionate yet truthful devotional-style book. It is meant to be a lighthearted, fun, and challenging compilation of suggestions and guidelines that we have put into practice, and in doing so, have found our MOYD.

As we wrote about various topics related to dating, God began to knit our hearts with whoever may someday hold our book in their hands. We prayed to God for you and are so thankful He led you to our book.

We hope your hearts will be stirred and filled with laughter. We also hope that you will have as much fun reading this book as we have had writing it. If you've made some mistakes in dating, NO WORRIES! The truth is, we've all been there at one point or another and there is absolutely no judgment. Those mistakes *do not define* you—they actually have the potential to *transform* you.

William Shakespeare is the author of the most famous love story ever told, *Romeo & Juliet.* Have you ever heard of his famous quote, "The world is your oyster?" It is often said to young people who are about to embark on life's journey. It means you can have anything this world has to offer. No dream is too big. You may even find a valuable pearl inside of your oyster! *Meet MOYD* is like that oyster containing many pearls of wisdom that we want to pass along to you. God has so many great things planned for your life with MOYD and we want to help you get there. Finding the person you want to spend the rest of your life with is no small endeavor.

In this book of advice, you will learn how to be confident in who you are, learn the pitfalls of dating, and find your happily ever after to name a few. At the end of the day, we all want to be loved. Our hope and prayer is that this book of advice encourages, challenges, and helps you to become the best version of yourself and ultimately leads you to the Man Of

Your Dreams—your MOYD! This book has the potential to change the course of your life forever.

We wish we had a treasure book of wisdom like this to guide us through our single years. Before we embark on finding MOYD, we need to learn how to see ourselves the way God sees us. The world is your oyster is a common phrase but many people forget the second half of that quote "...which I with sword will open." God has not only led you to this book but He has given you a sword to unlock all of the wisdom and blessings He has to offer, it's the Sword of the Spirit— His Holy Word.

God wants to write your love story and it will be a story that will blow Romeo and Juliet right out of the water!

Love, Cherie & Lona

You're Invited

We recognize that you may not believe in God. We tailored our book for all single ladies, both Christian and non-Christian. We don't consider this book to be religious however, this book has been inspired by our faith. Our faith has been tested many times throughout various trials we have walked through.
We have gained wisdom from our journey and have drawn foundational truths from God's Word.
Whether you believe in God or not,
please keep an open mind as you read this book.
We personally have experienced God in very tangible ways and hope this book will ultimately
draw your heart to His Son, Jesus. As we have learned, there is no greater love than the love God has for us.

"For God so loved the world that He gave His only son, that whoever believes in Him shall not perish but have everlasting life."
John 3:16

We live in a fallen world where sin exists and we all struggle with sin. Jesus came to pay the price for the sins of the world. He died so that we may live forever. If you weren't raised in church or do not have a personal relationship with Jesus,
would you like to invite Him into your heart today?
You may not know Him personally, but He sure does know you!
The day He formed you in His hands,
He marveled over the wonder of you! He loves you so much and desires a personal relationship with you.
You don't have to be perfect to follow Jesus, just be willing.
We invite you to simply pray these words:

*"Dear Jesus, come into my heart and please forgive me of my sins.
I desire to have a relationship with You.
I surrender my life to You this day."*
In Jesus' name, Amen

Chapter 1

Thoughts about Yourself

"For as she thinks in her heart, so is she."
Proverbs 23:7

Before you meet "MOYD" it is vital to have an understanding of who you are and where you come from. When most people hear this idea, they immediately think of the city where they were born. Perhaps they think of their nationality and family heritage. For instance, we draw a lot of who we are from our Italian culture and our family upbringing. It is wonderful to draw from all of these things, but we are talking about something so much deeper. We are talking about the moment you were actually thought of by God Himself.

Did you know that God thought of you before you were ever conceived? Eugene H. Peterson said it best in his book called *The Message*. He said, *"Long before He [God] laid down earth's foundations, He had us in mind, had settled on us as the focus of His love, to be made whole and holy by his love. Long, long ago He decided to adopt us into His family through Jesus Christ. (What pleasure He took in planning this!) He wanted us to enter into the celebration of his lavish gift-giving by the hand of His beloved Son." Ephesians 1:3-6*

God thinks the world of you so what do you think? The way you think about yourself has a huge effect on the way others think of you, including MOYD! So think good thoughts about yourself!

We compiled a list of the ones we feel are the most important. Some of these items were adapted from Dr. Neil T. Anderson's bookmark, "Who I am in Christ." You can also visit www.ficm.org (Freedom in Christ Ministries) for some great free resources.

1.   You were formed in the hands of God before He ever placed you in your mother's womb. *"Before I formed you in the womb, I knew you..." (Jeremiah 1:5a NIV)*
2.   Before you were born God set you apart.
3.   You were made in the image of God, full of unique talents and abilities.

2

4. You are loved, treasured, cherished, and accepted as a daughter of God.

5. Jesus Christ paid the ultimate price of death for your life; therefore, YOU ARE OF GREAT VALUE.

6. When you struggle with thoughts that say you are rejected, alone, abandoned, worthless, hopeless, inadequate, and insignificant, you should know that you are listening to the wrong voice.

7. You are chosen.

8. You are never alone.

9. You are not rejected.

10. You are not abandoned.

11. You are highly favored.

12. Your life is not hopeless.

13. You are stronger than you think.

14. You are braver than you know.

15. You are significant and your life plays an important role in this life.

16. You are not perfect, and neither is MOYD!

17. You are beautiful just as you are. All sizes, shapes, and colors are beautiful.

18. True beauty comes from within.

19. You are not single because you lack beauty, charm, or some miraculous quality.

20. You are not lacking something if you do not have a husband.

21. Unlike the famous movie quote from "Jerry Maguire," having a husband does NOT complete you.

22. Your words are powerful. Proverbs 18:21 says, *"Death and life are in the power of the tongue, and those who love it will eat its fruits.*

Thoughts About Yourself

Roadmap to MOYD:

1. What do you love about yourself?

_____

_____

_____

_____

2. Do you have negative thoughts about yourself? If so, write them here.

_____

_____

_____

_____

3. Now write the exact opposite of those negative words here.

_____

_____

_____

_____

5

4. Were there any items in the list above that you do not believe about yourself or that you are struggling to believe about yourself? If yes, write them here.

    _____

    _____

    _____

    _____

5. If you could make some changes about the negative thoughts you are believing, what would those changes be?

    _____

    _____

    _____

    _____

From Chelona Mama's heart...

It's painful to wait for MOYD, but he will be worth the wait. The waiting room is like a "refiner's fire." A refiner's fire refers to the process that raw gold goes through to purify its contents. When placed in the fire, any foreign metals will rise to the surface. This is called the "dross." The refiner will skim the dross off the top and what is left is the purest form of gold. It's a lengthy process but the final result leaves you with the most valuable form of gold that you could ever imagine.

It's time to heat the fire and refine the way we think about ourselves and the way we talk about ourselves. Let's skim the "dross" of negative words off of our minds. Remember, our words are very powerful, and they can literally shape our lives. When you believe the truth about who you truly are, you will drown out the negative thoughts. You'll be amazed by how much better you feel and that will spill over into how you act and react to any situation and will positively affect every relationship that you have, including MOYD. So choose to speak uplifting, encouraging words over yourself and others and see what awesome changes will happen in your life.

We all think negative thoughts throughout our lives. If you have trouble believing positive thoughts about yourself, it's ok. Start with baby steps in faith and pray the following prayer.

Dear Jesus,

Forgive me for speaking
negative words about myself.
Please help me to see myself
the way you see me.
Help me to see that I am
the apple of Your eye.
Show me how You love me
when I can't seem to love
myself.
In Jesus' name,
Amen

Chapter 2

Do's & Don'ts of Life

"Whoever gives heed to instruction prospers,
and blessed is the one who trusts in the LORD.
The wise in heart are called discerning,
and gracious words promote instruction."
Proverbs 16:20-30

In the last chapter, we spoke about how important the thoughts you have towards yourself affect you and everyone around you. In this chapter, we address a basic concept of how to approach life, carry yourself, and treat others. You may be questioning "Why do I have to work on myself so much? Just give me the formula to find my perfect guy already!" But the way you live your life, carry yourself, and treat others *will* attract that perfect guy! Trust the process. You may have already put most or all of the attributes below into practice. If so—GREAT JOB! Let this list be a reminder. Remember, these are simply guidelines to help you make a great first impression. You don't have to be perfect or lie about who you are. We want you to be your authentic self with healthy guardrails. Guardrails are here to protect you, not to boss you around or rob you of having fun. Psalm 16:6 says, *"The boundary lines have fallen for me in pleasant places; surely I have a delightful inheritance."*

1. Be teachable.
2. Think before you speak. *"The heart of the wise teaches his mouth and adds learning to his lips. "Pleasant words are like a honeycomb, Sweetness to the soul and health to the bones." (Proverbs 16:23-24 NKJV)*
3. Be kind. Be as beautiful on the inside as you are on the outside.
4. As we mentioned in the last chapter, words have power. You are what you say you are, so speak kindly about yourself and others.
5. Don't put yourself down. By saying you are too "fat" or too "skinny" or "ugly" or "dumb" is basically speaking "poison" over yourself.

6. When you speak it out loud, your ears hear it and your mind will believe it, so speak positive, life-giving words over yourself.

This next section refers to "Mixed Company," such as your co-workers and peers, or anyone who is in authority over you such as your teacher, coach, boss, Pastor, Rabbi, or Priest! We want to encourage you to be the best version of yourself when you are around people because it is possible, they may be the very ones who will introduce you to MOYD!

7. Don't be too much too soon. You don't have to reveal your whole self or every aspect of your life over a cup of coffee. In time, they will get to know you and all of the wonderful things about you, all in good time.

8. Before you blow your "trouser trumpet" in front of mixed company, you REALLY need to be sure that the guy you are dating is ok with potty humor! While some people are comfortable with potty humor, some are not. Passing gas (aka farting, blowing the trouser trumpet, tooting, pooting and I'm sure there are many other

13

names for it) can sometimes be a major turn-off for certain types of guys.

9. *"Do not let unwholesome [foul, profane, worthless, vulgar] words ever come out of your mouth, but only such speech as is good for building up others, according to the need and the occasion, so that it will be a blessing to those who hear [you speak]."* (Ephesians 4:29 Amplified Bible AMP)

10. Therefore, try not to say the F word, B word, Sh word, or any other bad cuss words in front of mixed company. ☺ Just want to be honest here, God knows we are not immune to letting a bad word slip here and there. Everybody says a cuss word once in a while. What we have come to realize is that bad words are like pouring mud on a beautiful flower. Why would we want to do that in front of mixed company, especially when it's a first impression?!

11. Like the 3rd Ten Commandment says, *"You shall not take the name of the Lord your God in vain."* (Exodus 20:7 NKJV)
Don't tell dirty jokes.

12. Try not to laugh at dirty jokes.

13. Be careful what you read, watch, and listen to. What you read, what you watch, and what you listen to gets inside of you and overflows out of you in various ways.

14. *"Above all else, guard your heart, for everything you do flows from it." (Proverbs 4:23 NIV)*

This next section is about our greatest enemy, Satan. Whether you believe in him or not, there is evil in this world. We know from the beginning of time, there has been a dark presence that exists in the world ever since the fall of mankind in the Garden of Eden. You can find this account in Genesis chapters two and three. Please try not to do anything that opens your mind and spirit up to that dark world. We know that Satan is real. He loves to wreak havoc in our lives. This is why we should always guard our minds. If you see horror movies, you can not un-see those images. When you are single and you live alone, you won't be alone for long! Freddie, Chucky, and Jason will be stuck in your mind. Every single sound in your apartment will scare the heck out of you.

15. Do not go see horror movies.

16. Don't go to fortune tellers.

17. Abstain from participating in any "seances," "witchcraft" or "occult" practices.

18. Don't get drunk. It's not a sin to have an alcoholic beverage but when you become drunk, it lowers your inhibitions, and you may behave recklessly. *"Do not get drunk on wine, which leads to debauchery. Instead, be filled with the Spirit." (Ephesians 5:18 NIV)*

19. Do not do drugs. When you are high and wasted, your guard is down. LADIES, we all know NOTHING good happens when our guards are down!

20. Drugs and alcohol are addictive and once you start participating in these activities it is nearly impossible to stop craving them.

21. For several reasons, avoid vaping or smoking anything. Both contain nicotine which is highly addictive and can cause heart problems. Smoking also causes lung cancer. Besides killing you sooner, smoking can stain your teeth and both vaping and smoking give you bad breath! Nobody wants to kiss the lips of someone with rancid breath.

22. Don't dive in too fast. Don't say I love you right after meeting someone. Remember, love takes time.

23. Ask God to give you an abundance of common sense and wisdom. (If you really want to be wise, read Proverbs 😊) Wisdom protects you. Always use wisdom.

24. Keep your passwords, PIN number, and bank account numbers to yourself.

25. Do not be overly trusting in any relationship.

26. Trust takes time and must be earned.

27. Be willing to obey God, He knows and wants what is best for you. Sometimes it will cost you something precious to obey Him but no matter what, we promise it will be worth it in the end. Nobody will want better for your life than God.

28. Learn the true meaning of LOVE from 1 Corinthians 13. This is how God defines love and we appreciate the simplicity of the following version by Eugene H. Peterson from I Corinthians 13:4-7 *The Message*:

Love never gives up.
Love cares more for others than for self.
Love doesn't want what it doesn't have.
Love doesn't strut,
Doesn't have a swelled head,
Doesn't force itself on others,
Isn't always "me first,"
Doesn't fly off the handle,
Doesn't keep score of the sins of others,
Doesn't revel when others grovel,
Takes pleasure in the flowering of truth,
Puts up with anything,
Trusts God always,
Always looks for the best,
Never looks back,
But keeps going to the end

Roadmap to MOYD:

1. Do you have any regrets? If so, list them here:

   _____

   _____

   _____

   _____

   _____

2. What were some of the negative consequences you experienced from those regrets?

   _____

   _____

   _____

   _____

   _____

3. If you could go back in time and erase some of those regrets, would you?

    YES or NO _____

    If yes, what would you do

    differently?_____

    _____

    _____

    _____

    _____

4. We know that we cannot change the past, but we certainly have the power to change the future. Write down some of the things you will do differently. Everything you change will affect your future.

    _____

    _____

    _____

    _____

    _____

From Chelona Mama's heart...

It's ok to have regrets. Every single one of us has regrets. We have all made mistakes from time to time and still do! Owning your mistakes is a sign of authenticity and maturity. For one to have no regrets would suggest one has lived a perfect life. No one has lived a perfect life. Your past does not have to dictate your future. Anyone can turn their life around at any moment. It just takes surrender, action, and a sincere heart.

Would you like to turn back the clock right now and wipe the slate clean? Do you ever wonder about Heaven? Do you know that Jesus died on the cross to pay for all of your regrets, mistakes, and sins? It is as simple as asking Him to forgive you of your sins and come into your heart. This is a gift that God gave to you and me. He loves you so much that He sent His only son Jesus to die for you. John 3:16 says, *"For God so loved the world, that He gave His only Son, so that everyone who believes in Him will not perish, but have eternal life."* We would love to see you someday in Heaven. God gave you free will, the choice is up to you.

MEET MOYD

If you missed the invitation page at the beginning of the book, we would be so honored to walk you through this! Simply pray the following prayer.

Dear Jesus,

Come into my heart and
Forgive me for all of my
past mistakes.
Help me to listen to the
Holy Spirit.
Give me the strength to
forgive myself.
I believe You have the best life
planned for me for my future.
I surrender my whole life to you,
every single part.
In Jesus' name,
Amen

Chapter 3

Friendships and Relationships

"Greater love has no one than this:
to lay down one's life for one's friends."
John 15:13

Sometimes the best way to meet MOYD is through family and friendships. Life is all about relationships but sometimes they are extremely challenging to maintain. We thought it might be helpful to have a list of things that we have learned along the way through the ups and downs of our own relationships. Remember, every relationship walks through seasons of love and happiness and also seasons of turmoil and troubles. You are not the only one with family drama or soap opera friendships. You are not alone. We are in this together. God can restore broken relationships, but it requires work on our part. Are you ready? Let's go!!!

1.   God has a tribe of people for you but sometimes it is very difficult to find that tribe. Be patient and look for people who will lift you up when you are down. Good friends will make time for you, challenge you, and will have a positive impact on your life. Use discernment when trying to decide who to open up to. Sometimes people can be good listeners, but they can also be big talkers 😑. Make sure you discern who you can trust with the information of your heart.

2.   Good friends will enrich your life and not drag you into a pit of despair.

3.   Jesus is the greatest friend you will ever have. *"One who has unreliable friends soon comes to*

ruin, but there is a friend who sticks closer than a brother." (*Proverbs 18:24 NIV*)

4. Treasure and cherish your friends and family by spending quality time with them.

5. Beware of offense. Sometimes we get so offended over little things but don't sweat the small stuff. Keep it in perspective.

6. If someone hurts you, you should go directly to them and tell them in a loving way how they have hurt you. *"If your brother or sister sins, go and point out their fault, just between the two of you. If they listen to you, you have won them over. But if they will not listen, take one or two others along, so that every matter may be established by the testimony of two or three witnesses."* (*Matthew 18:15-16 NIV*)

7. Don't gossip to everyone else about your offense.

8. Give people grace because you never know what they are walking through. Most of the time, if people are doing something hurtful, it has more to do with what they are going through and surprisingly has NOTHING to do with you.

9. FORGIVE, FORGIVE, FORGIVE!

10. To forgive does not justify their wrong behavior, but it does release you from resentment and bitterness. These things will have a negative effect on you if you do not forgive. Forgiveness frees us from their control. It breaks the tether of the thing that hurt us. We waste so much precious time and energy brooding over the situation when we can put all of that time and energy into doing something positive that will help our lives and others.

11. Seek to understand first before being

understood. Give the benefit of the doubt. Don't assume you know why they did what they did (refer back to #8).

12. Be a good communicator.

13. Always honor your mother and your father. This is the fifth commandment— "Honor (respect, obey, care for) your father and your mother, so that your days may be prolonged in the land the Lord your God gives you." *(Exodus 20:12 AMP)*

14. Make an effort to call your family because they were the first ones to know you and love you.

15. Refrain from trying to get info about MOYD from his family. Their loyalty is to him not to you.

16. Remember the birthdays of those you love.

17. Don't trust everyone you meet. Trust is earned over time.

18. Try not to unload all of your problems on all of your friends. Only share with your closest circle of friends who have proven to be trustworthy.

19. Don't be a complainer. If you complain a lot, you will be known as a "complainer." When you die, do you know what you will be remembered for? —You guessed it, "complaining!"

20. Don't forget to ask about *their* life. Healthy conversations are a tennis match, not a one-way street.

21. Do not spend the entire evening talking all about yourself.

22. Always put others before yourself.

23. Do not let people take advantage of you. Don't be a doormat.

24. Healthy boundaries are good because they provide a bridge of communication but putting up walls will hurt your relationships. Walls will ultimately isolate you from the world.

25. Be nice and be kind.

26. Be a great listener.

27. Serve your family and your friends.

28. Say "Yes" to the bridesmaid dress! Serve at someone's wedding and you may meet your husband there! We were bridesmaids before we were brides! *(From Cherie—that's where I met my husband! We actually walked together in a wedding and 11 months later, we were married in the very same place we met. I nearly missed this opportunity because I almost declined to be a bridesmaid at that wedding! But I said yes, and it was the best decision I have ever made! It was a whirlwind of a love story that I will share later in the book.*

Roadmap to MOYD:

1. Do you easily forgive, or do you find it challenging to forgive? Please explain.

   _____

   _____

   _____

   _____

   _____

2. If there is anyone in your life that you have yet to forgive, list them here. (*Be honest! If you need more paper, grab it now!*)

   _____

   _____

   _____

   _____

   _____

3. Are you able to forgive without them apologizing first or making any attempt to make things right?

_____

_____

_____

_____

_____

4. We know this may sound morbid, but if those people died suddenly, what would be your biggest regret? What would you have done differently?

_____

_____

_____

_____

_____

Then go do it now! Do the hard thing, lay down the hurt, work it out, and heal your relationship. You will never regret it. Even if they don't respond how you want them to, do it anyway. God will bless you for it!

From Chelona Mama's heart...

Sometimes, with a broken relationship, all it takes is a simple "I'm sorry." Pride is usually the main reason why someone does not apologize. We know it's sometimes difficult to admit when we are wrong but holding onto pride can ruin your life. Unforgiveness eventually breeds bitterness like a field of grass laced with a bunch of weeds. We know that weeds choke out healthy flowering plants and beautiful grass. They rob nutrients from the soil which means your flowers won't be able to grow to their full potential. Weeds steal the water that your flowering plants need in order to thrive. Consequently, bitterness robs you of your joy. It has the potential to overtake you and can change who you are. Bitterness will keep you from thriving and you won't be able to reach your full potential if you stay bitter. Bitterness affects every aspect of your life, including your relationships as well as your journey to MOYD. We encourage you to make a decision right now to FORGIVE the ones who have hurt you.

The Bible says in Proverbs 16:18, *"Pride goes before destruction, a haughty spirit before a fall."* This is why we need the Holy Spirit. It is that still small voice that speaks truth to our hearts. The Holy Spirit will help us in our relationships. The Holy Spirit will give us the words and actions that we need to repair the brokenness.

Pray the following prayer over your situation and see what God can do!

Dear God,

Please help me to be
a good family member and friend
through your Holy Spirit. Please help me to
forgive the ones who have offended me. I
know that holding onto unforgiveness
leads to bitterness. This is not who I am
— this is not who I want to become.
Help me to seek forgiveness from those
whom I have hurt. Please give me the
courage to overcome my pride
and fix whatever is broken in my
relationships.
I understand that I was created to
love people the way you do.
Help me to see others through your eyes,
In Jesus' name,
Amen

Chapter 4

For Such a Time as This...

And the king loved Esther more than any of the other young women. He was so delighted with her that he set the royal crown on her head and declared her Queen..."
Esther 2:17

Have you ever read the book of Esther in the Bible? It is one of our favorite stories! It's about the most unlikely, young, Jewish, orphan becoming the Queen of Persia! King Ahasuerus is in search of a new Queen and invites young women from every province of his realm to the palace. A feast of exotic cuisine was prepared for them, and they were given beauty treatments as preparation to present themselves before the King. These beauty treatments were nothing like our day at the spa. *"Each young woman's turn came to go into King Ahasuerus after she had completed twelve months' preparation, according to the regulations for the women, for thus were the days of their preparation apportioned: six months with oil of myrrh, and six months with perfumes and preparations for beautifying women. Thus prepared, each young woman went to the king, and she was given whatever she desired to take with her from the women's quarters to the king's palace." Esther 2:12-13 (NKJV)*

Here is a really interesting fact about Esther. She could've had anything she wanted from the palace, but she listened to the advice of Hegai, who was in charge of preparing all of these beautiful women to meet the King. As a result, Esther was highly favored by the King. It goes on to say, *"So he set a royal crown on her head and made her queen instead of Vashti. And the king gave a great banquet, Esther's banquet, for all his nobles and officials. He proclaimed a holiday throughout the provinces and distributed gifts with royal liberality." Esther 2:17-18 NIV*

Doesn't that sound like the most amazing story? There are so many plot twists and turns, even a murder plot—but we won't spoil it for you! Read the story of Esther and get prepared to meet MOYD! He may not be a King, but if you treat him like royalty,

MOYD will do the same for you. Ladies, it's not all about your beauty, but the truth is, that men are different from women, they are more visual in their attractions, more so than women.

With this in mind, we thought it would be helpful and fun to list some tips below. Consider us your very own personal stylist, beauty, and health coach. We understand, of course, that everyone has a different regimen for caring for their bodies. The advice below is from our personal experience, and certainly not exhaustive. You may already be doing most or all of the items we've listed and we're sure you can probably give us your own great advice from your personal experience too! If most of the list is new information to you, we hope you will put some of these tips into practice. We pray God will shine the light of favor on you just like He did for Queen Esther! Ok girls let's have some fun!

Body care tips:
1. Take a long bubble bath when you have the time and put some essential oils in the tub. It's always good to smell your best and take care of your skin so it doesn't dry out. It's so relaxing and therapeutic too!

2. If your skin is looking dry and ashy, use sugar scrubs for the body! (Cherie) My favorite one is the eucalyptus & spearmint sugar scrub from Bath & Body Works. It leaves your skin feeling soft and silky. You can also use exfoliating gloves.

3. Put moisturizer or Vaseline on your elbows, knees, and feet at night because these areas can get extremely dry and rough. (Lona) Also, cut a lemon in half and massage the inside of the lemon on these areas. Leave on for 10 minutes, then wash off with lukewarm water. This exfoliates and lightens the skin. As we age, these areas can become darker.

4. We know it's a real pain, but keep those armpits and legs shaved or waxed! For all you "ell-naturelle" girls, hairy pits do increase body odor. Nobody likes stubble and no guy likes a girl who smells stinky!

5. Speaking of smells, we love perfumes and body sprays but not everyone loves the same scent as you do so use it sparingly. (Cherie) I remember back in high school; I had a friend who wore a perfume laced with patchouli and I loathed that scent. To this day, patchouli makes

me nauseous. I have another friend who cannot be around any perfume whatsoever. No matter how beautiful it smells, she gets queasy every time!

6. If you invest in a pricy perfume, a little goes a long way. Perfume is usually very strong and one or two squirts on the neck and wrist are usually enough.

7. (Cherie) I love essential oils and all of their amazing properties. However, sometimes people take it too far. I know there are healing properties in various essential oils, but to the girls who think essential oils are literally "Jesus-in-a-bottle," and over-using them, think twice about using them as your daily perfume. If you are wearing rosemary and oregano, be aware that some people think you smell like a Thanksgiving turkey or a pizza! I like both of those things, but do I want my body to smell like that? NO! I prefer anything fruity and flowery myself! I hate to admit this, but I know someone who wears so much rosemary and oregano at the same time, that when she hugs me, I walk away smelling like her! I don't want to smell like a turkey.

Skincare for the Face, Nail Care &
Oral Hygiene Tips:

8. Always wear sunscreen, especially on your face!

9. Make sure you take good care of your face beginning in your teen years. Don't use face products that have a fragrance. Stick with a basic skincare line. Some dermatologists recommend Cetaphil, Cerave, and Purpose. (Cherie) These products are not fancy and not expensive, but I have found them to be the best for my complexion. (Lona) My favorite skincare lines are Neutrogena and Oil of Olay.

10. Try not to pop a pimple! Don't touch it because natural oils exist on your fingertips. Touching the pimple will make it worse! If you wake up with "Pluto" on your face—get a clean washcloth, wet it with a warm compress, and put it on the pimple. This will help reduce inflammation. Also, put a small amount of Cerave Salicylic Acid Acne Treatment Gel on the pimple and leave it alone! This will help clear the pimple as well as prevent breakouts. Benzoyl peroxide and retinol are other acne treatment options. Check with your dermatologist who will recommend which products will work best for you. (Lona) In my teen

years, I put toothpaste with baking soda on my pimples as an acne hack and it made them diminish too!

11. If you are in your 20s, please make sure you use a good moisturizer on your face daily. Once the wrinkles appear, it can be difficult to make them disappear.

12. For those of you over 40, it's good to wash your face with a gentle exfoliating scrub such as the one made by Clinique.

13. We are learning how to age gracefully. While we hate some of the changes that come with aging, we also have to remember that those expression lines are from a life well lived. Nevertheless, always use a moisturizer.

14. When drinking from a straw, put the straw on the side of your mouth, not in the front. This will help you to avoid causing wrinkles on the upper lip.

15. Speaking of upper lips, if you are starting to resemble Mario or Luigi, get that mustache waxed!

16. Pluck, wax, or thread your eyebrows if necessary. And try not to over-tweeze them. (Lona) I'll never forget the first time I had my eyebrows professionally sculpted. I could not

believe what a difference it made! I felt like I was able to wear less eye shadow and mascara. The sculpting really complimented the shape of my eyes. You can maintain them yourself after you have a professional sculpt them for you. If you have sparse eyebrows or none at all, you can have your eyebrows tinted or tattooed.

17. When looking at your phone remember to relax your eyebrows, otherwise, you will end up with "angry bird" lines between your brows!

18. There is some debate as to whether or not you should wax "other parts" of your body—whether you are a beauty queen or free-spirited hippie — we will leave that one up to you;) OUCH!

19. Moving on—Get your nails done girls! Be you. Be creative or be simple, just make sure your nails and toes are all prettied up! Some guys love a girl with pretty nails and cute toes! Even if you only like natural nails, it is important to keep your cuticles pushed back and your nails manicured so that you don't get hangnails.

20. Try to manage your stress. Mayoclinic.org says, *"Uncontrolled stress can make your skin more sensitive and trigger acne breakouts and other skin problems. To encourage healthy skin and a*

healthy state of mind take steps to manage your stress. Get enough sleep, set reasonable limits, scale back your to-do list, and make time to do the things you enjoy. The results might be more dramatic than you expect."

21. Don't smoke. Mayoclinic.org also says, *"Smoking makes your skin look older and contributes to wrinkles. Smoking narrows the tiny blood vessels in the outermost layers of skin, which decreases blood flow and makes skin paler. This also depletes the skin of oxygen and nutrients that are important to skin health."*

22. How's your smile? There are many ways to keep your smile sparkly with toothpaste and treatments. You don't want them to look unnaturally white, but you don't want them to be badly stained either. We also recommend regular dental checkups every six months. This is not only to produce a beautiful smile, but it also prevents tooth decay and gum disease—oral hygiene can also affect other areas of your body as well.

Hair and Makeup Tips:

23. Shampoo, condition, and style your hair to keep it from smelling weird or looking greasy. It

doesn't have to look perfect all the time—a messy bun is very cute!

24. (Lona) I personally love Kenra, Joico, Redken, and Olaplex hair products and have used my tried-and-true Sebastian Shaper hairspray ever since I was a teenager.

25. (Cherie) From one curly-haired girl to another— if you have naturally curly hair, invest in some products that tame those frizzies! I love Paul Mitchell Awapuii shampoo and detangler, and John Frieda mousse and gel for the ends. Another one of my favorite products is grooming creme by Kenra. It smells like candy! Most importantly, you must also have a good diffuser on your blow dryer. Never brush through dry curly hair unless you are about to wash it. It will be a frizzy mess! Never run your fingers through wet hair while blow drying because you are basically stretching out the curl and it will look wiry instead of curly. I always flip my hair upside down and scrunch it with my hands while I blow dry with a diffuser on the end. This step creates a coil-like curl and it gives your hair body!

26. You are so incredibly lovely without any makeup. If you decide to wear some, makeup should

always enhance your natural beauty. A little mascara, lip gloss, and light rosy cheeks go a long way! Unless you have noticeable skin problems, I would avoid wearing foundation for as long as you can! Less is always better.

27. If you like dramatic eyes, go for a nude lip.

28. If you love wearing red lipstick, go for something really simple on the eyes—some light brown or nude eyeshadow or maybe some light mascara.

29. Who doesn't love a shimmery, glittery eyeshadow? We do—go for it! However, as we age, our skin becomes a bit more "textured" and shimmery eyeshadows accentuate that texture. We don't want that! Here's our best advice. If you are over 40, keep the shimmery eyeshadows off of your upper lid. A little pop of glitter right above your lashes or some shimmer in the corners is always pretty.

30. We love false eyelashes—they are so fancy! But we suggest making sure that your false eyelashes are just a little bit fuller and just slightly longer than your natural lashes. When women wear extra-long, super thick, jet-black lashes, they almost look like little baby tarantulas on their eyes! The more natural the better unless

of course, it's New Year's Eve or a special occasion where you can go a little more dramatic and bolder with your look!

31. Stay on top of the latest makeup trends. If you are still sporting that blue eye shadow from the '70s or royal blue eyeliner from the '80s, make sure that era has come back around! This is also true with fashion. Check the latest fashion magazines for the most up-to-date advice.

32. Also, regarding fashion, it is important to dress for your body type. There are many different body shapes such as rectangle, round, pear, and triangle. You can research great resources online to help you determine what fashion looks best for your body type. You will also find what colors compliment you the most.

33. Always remember the most important beauty and fashion tip of all time—keep it classy, not trashy!

Health & Fitness

1. You are beautiful no matter what size you are, but we all need to do whatever it takes to make sure that we are in our absolute best health. Go to the doctor for your annual physical, and most

of all, don't forget your yearly visit to the gynecologist. Get that mammogram and protect your "ta-ta's"— no excuses!

2. If you are attracted to athletic men, you should get involved in some athletic activities. First of all, it's great for your body to keep moving no matter what age you are. Secondly, you may just meet MOYD at the gym, or the pool, or the track—so go work out, swim, or run your little heart out! JUST KEEP MOVING!

3. Remember this important rule about food: "If you can't pronounce it, don't put it inside your body!" Always read the labels on foods. It is best to buy foods that have the least amount of added preservatives. Fresh is always best.

4. Eat more fruits, vegetables, fish, and whole grains, and reduce processed sugar and white flour.

5. Don't skip breakfast. Choose a food full of protein to get that day started and your metabolism going!

6. Beware of emotional attachments to foods or beverages.

   a. (Cherie) I love sweet tea, probably because I've been drinking it since I was a toddler. It has always been and still is my #1 drink choice. Sweet tea reminds me of the most important woman in my life, my mother Cheryl. I must confess, I have an emotional attachment to sweet tea. When I'm happy I want it, when I'm stressed out or sad, I especially want it! It reminds me of my childhood filled with iridescent glitter, red birds, and rainbows when life seemed so simple and innocent. It reminds me of hot summers when we visited my Aunt Janice and Uncle Bobby's house in the deep woods on those old, orange clay roads of South Georgia. I can still see myself swinging on their front porch and sipping that freshly boiled sweet tea out of a glass jar as hummingbirds fluttered around me with the sweet scent of the Georgia pine tree air. I love this memory, but I need to be careful not to drink too much sweet tea.

b. Any food or drink used to make us feel better can become a problem. If it becomes an hourly or daily habit it could become an addiction. Sugar, caffeine, alcohol, and tobacco products have the potential to curb your cravings and your body becomes dependent on them. Too much of anything is usually not the healthiest choice for your body. Remember the Bible says, *"Your body is a temple of the Holy Spirit."* We all need to make a conscious decision to have self-control so we can live to the fullest all the days of our lives. Again, we're not saying deny yourself of the things you love most, we're saying treat your favorite food or beverage like a reward. When you have a really good week, get out that big glass of sweet tea and lick the glass clean—Enjoy it!

c. Remove all fake sweeteners from your diet. No pink, blue, yellow, or green packet of sweetener contains anything actually good for your body. These items are difficult for your body to break down. Replace all the diet sodas and anything containing fake additives with water. According to the Mayo Clinic, your body is made up of approximately 60% water and we lose 8–12 cups of water per day! All of our major organs need water, and it is up to us to replace that water daily. Get yourself a large, pretty stainless-steel travel cup and fill it with ice and water. Keep it with you at all times and take it everywhere you go. Trust us, after a week of this, you will find yourself actually craving water instead of the fake drinks.

Roadmap to MOYD:

1. Do you agree it is important to prepare yourself for MOYD in the various ways listed above? If not, why?

_____

_____

_____

_____

2. What advice listed above inspired you to begin a new day-to-day regimen?

_____

_____

_____

_____

3. Is there any advice that you disagree with? If yes, what would you do differently?

_____

_____

_____

_____

4. What daily activity is the most difficult for you to do on a regular basis?

_____

_____

_____

_____

5. Do you have any emotional attachments to food or drinks? If yes, list them here.

_____

_____

_____

_____

6. What do you think you will do differently after reading the above tips?

_____

_____

_____

_____

7. Who's going shopping after reading this chapter? LOL _____

From Chelona Mama's heart...

So far, we have discussed what you think about yourself, the do's and don'ts of life, and friendships and relationships. We thought it would be a perfect time to have some fun with beauty tips and caring for your body. It has been quite a journey so far. I know at times you may have felt like some of this is too much, but we love you enough to be really honest with you—just like a good mama should. In this book, you have learned from the things we have done right in our lives, but you have also learned from the wisdom we have gained from our mistakes. Some of these beauty tips are techniques, products, and regimens that we are just now learning and are trying to put into practice! We know this is sound advice, but we also know that sometimes, it's really difficult to deny yourself of all the yummy guilty pleasures of this world. We totally understand but trust us girls—it will be worth it.

MEET MOYD

We also want to remind you of something really important. You are beautiful no matter what size you are. Our recommendations aren't about size, they're about becoming the healthiest version of yourself. Our vision for you is to live a long, happy life here on Earth with MOYD and we will all meet someday, if not sooner, then definitely later in Heaven when this life is over. Please pray the following prayer.

Dear God,

Help me to set healthy practices for my body inside and out. Help me to love myself as much as you love me. Give me Your strength to overcome unhealthy habits. Allow me to see results quickly to inspire me to keep going. I am really excited to experience all the goodness you have for me as I trust you to help me prepare to meet the man of my dreams.

In Jesus' name,

Amen

Chapter 5

Do's & Don'ts of Dating

"Daughters...., I charge you: Do not arouse or awaken love until it so desire...Place me like a seal over your heart, like a seal on your arm; for love is as strong as death, its jealousy unyielding as the grave. It burns like blazing fire, like a mighty flame. Many waters cannot quench love; rivers cannot sweep it away."

Song of Solomon 8:4-7

Ladies, take a deep breath. This chapter is loaded with some excellent words of advice, but there is a lot to unpack. Remember, there is NO JUDGMENT. Our motive is to help and encourage you to be the best version of yourself at all times so you will attract your MOYD. We ourselves have broken some of the rules on this list and trust us, we suffered the consequences! But we are not going to throw ourselves under the bus just yet ☺.

Before you start reading, ask God to give you wisdom and guard your steps. Ask Him to reveal to you what needs to change in your life and what doesn't. Girls, we truly love each and every one of you reading this book. We hope God shows you that He has placed this book in your hands to encourage and equip you. You may already be putting many of the points below into practice. Wherever you are in your journey, highlight the ones that you need to work on and give yourself a gold star for every one of the points that you are achieving! Most of all, be encouraged and allow the words in this book to guide you. As you apply this advice to your life, you will become closer and closer to attracting the kind of man you've always been dreaming of! OK—let's do this!

1. Pray for MOYD. Ask God to lead him to you.
2. If you think you have met MOYD, do not make the first move.
3. Let him pursue you.
4. Do not assume every guy you meet is "the ONE!"
5. Do not act desperate.

6. Don't be too needy.

7. Don't talk over him when he's speaking.

8. Do not try to get MOYD's number.

9. Do not offer your number to MOYD.

10. Once again, let MOYD pursue you.

11. Be careful of the following regarding online dating apps:

- Don't be catfished and believe everything you see. The picture may not even be him, and some or all of his details may be lies.

- Research his online presence.

- Do not give him any personal information other than the limited information posted on your profile.

- Don't allow him to be pushy or manipulate you to date or communicate with him.

- Be ready for rejection or to be ghosted.

- Your options are unlimited, so you become too picky about every little thing without even meeting him. You swipe left because he has a big nose, but you may miss out on an amazing person.

- With millions of candidates online, your competition is overwhelming. This can lead to low self-esteem and insecurity.
- Beware of certain dating apps that have the reputation of being "booty-call" apps. While some dating apps are totally valid, others are used mostly for sex hook-ups so be careful.
- Apply all the general rules that we have listed for dating to online dating as well

12. Don't text MOYD. If the guy is really MOYD, he will text you first! It's totally fine to text him back but don't be the one initiating all of the communication. Some guys are sincerely nice guys and they do not want to hurt a girl's feelings so they simply text back thinking nothing of it but they don't honestly want to pursue the relationship. If he is acting disinterested, just let it go and stop texting him.

13. There are times when a girl gets a text from a guy and thinks "WOW, he is texting with me so he must really be into me!" Girls, listen to us carefully. Sometimes he is into you, but the truth is, a text message is not proof that he is actually

wanting to have a relationship with you. When MOYD is really into you, you will know it! It will be a lot more than a simple text.

14. Never text a "sexy picture" of yourself to a guy! A pretty picture of your face is cute and sweet! But DO NOT send sexy pictures of your body parts to a guy—never ever! Remember, these pics can be shared with anyone, posted on social media, printed, etc. Keep it covered, make them wonder!

15. No "sexting"- not ever! This is so detrimental to you both physically and mentally. Just like we mentioned in the last point, these pictures and videos can be shared with anyone, posted on social media, etc. (more about this subject in Chapter 6) Just ask yourself this question, *"Would I be able to share this with my mother?"* If the answer is no, don't share it. You are belittling yourself. You are worth more than this. He may act like sexting brings you closer but ask yourself, how many other sexy girl pictures does he have on his phone? Also, by doing this, you are showing him what kind of girl you are and it's NOT the marrying kind of girl. He will be thinking,

"If she is doing this with me, how many other guys has she done this with?"

16. Regarding Snapchat, you may think Snapchat is safe because it disappears immediately, but people can save those embarrassing photos or video SNAPS and use them against you.

17. Be extra careful what you post on social media. When you post, it is online forever. Even if you delete it, someone may have already copied it. (More about this subject in Chapter 6)

18. When you meet a potential MOYD, if he shows interest in you and wants to go out, suggest gathering with a group of friends in a public place. It is better to be safe than sorry!

19. Go for coffee. Keep it simple. Keep it brief.

20. Keep it light-hearted and have fun!

21. Allow him to open the door for you.

22. If things aren't going well on the date, plan an escape. Have your friend call you during the date and have a code word ready to let her know if everything is cool.

23. Be authentic.

24. Don't pretend to like his interests if you don't.

25. Don't talk about past boyfriends.

26. Don't try to control or manipulate him. Ok ladies—We all like to get our own way, don't we? We get it. But please try not to! Try to make the date enjoyable for both of you. Find activities, restaurants, and events that you BOTH will enjoy.

27. Too much too soon will ruin chances with MOYD. Just chill! We are not referring to only sexual, but also talking, texting, calling, or flirting to name a few.

28. Don't say I love you first, allow MOYD to lead your heart into LOVE.

29. Never chase a man, or you will be chasing him for life. The movie *My Best Friend's Wedding* is a prime example of this—check it out!

30. MOYD is a leader, and He likes to make the first move!

31. When the check comes, you should offer to pay for yourself, but honestly, the perfect gentleman will offer to pay for the whole bill.

32. It's not a good idea to date a guy who has dated your girlfriends. Why would you want to anyways? This only brings drama, drama, and more drama! You don't want to date another girl's leftovers.

33. If he cheated on her then he WILL cheat on you.

34. If a man rejects you, he is not the one. Let him go!

35. If a man verbally degrades you, He is NOT MOYD! Let him go!

36. If a man hits you, run as fast as you can and never look back. Do not give him a second chance. Report him to the police. An abuser does NOT deserve a second chance! Let him go!!! (The national domestic abuse hotline is 1-800-799-SAFE)

37. Do not believe that you can change a man! We do believe everyone has the ability to change, but only God can transform someone's heart. The only way a man will ever change is for him to get alone with God. Therefore, once again "LET HIM GO so GOD CAN DO HIS WORK!"

38. The little old church lady says, "Modest is hottest 🔥 mystery will make history."

39. Don't act sexy, act mysterious. Leave room for his imagination. Remember, mystery is very sexy. Always make a guy wonder.

40. Be confident, not cocky.

41. For those of you "Dolly Parton" gals, we understand that it is sometimes challenging to keep the "girls" under wraps, however, try not to show so much cleavage. MOYD will look forward to discovering that asset someday! Showing too much cleavage is like someone telling you how the movie ends before you actually get to see it! It spoils all the fun!!!

42. Give MOYD a treasure hunt to find!

43. Do not wear tight pants that display your 🐫. (If you can't figure this one out, ask a friend because we are not going to type the words 😳😵)

44. Just like Elsa sings "LET IT GO! LET IT GO!"— let go of those thin bras that display how cold it is! Showing off your frozen nipples will only attract the wrong kind of guy!

45. Always wear proper undergarments. Wear a good strong bra, otherwise, you will regret it by the time you're 50. If you wear a good bra, your ta-tas won't hang down to your knees!

46. We love cute dresses and shorts but no one needs to see butt cheeks hanging out the bottom. 😳

47. Again, leave some room for his imagination.

69

Well, wasn't that list a load of fun? Please answer the questions below honestly and make any changes necessary. We're praying for you and cheering you on every step of the way!

Roadmap to MOYD

1. If there are any points from the above list that make you want to roll your eyes and scream "Whatever!" please write those here:

   _____

   _____

   _____

   _____

   (Did we give you enough space? LOL)

2. What changes will you make in the future regarding any of the points above? And why do you feel like you have to make those changes?

   _____

   _____

   _____

   _____

3. What practices will you start to implement from the list above that you haven't done yet?

_____

_____

_____

_____

_____

_____

_____

4. If any items on the above list seem impossible for you to implement into your life, please write them here. Just ask God to show you what to do and He will!

_____

_____

_____

_____

_____

_____

_____

From Lona...

I remember distinctly where and when I prayed for my MOYD. I was only 18 years old, in my jammies talking with God in bed before I fell asleep. I remember feeling sad and frustrated over my current relationship and was sick of playing games. I wanted my Prince Charming, my happily ever after, my *forever*. At that moment, I felt like if I didn't meet my husband before my boyfriend returned from college, I knew I would end up with my boyfriend. He was a hard, bad habit to break. (Cue the 1984 *Chicago 17* vinyl!) And I promise you girls, all it took was that ONE prayer. It still amazes me how quickly He answered. Two weeks later, God led me to my husband Jim on a hayride through the college and career class at my church. Let me simply say, that a good church is an <u>excellent</u> place to find your MOYD. Jim is truly the man of my dreams. If I hadn't prayed and asked God to bring me my husband, I believe I would've settled for less than God's best for me. Girls trust me, you **never** want to settle for anything less than God's best! God knows you better than yourself and knows exactly what you need in a man, even when you don't. God loves you so much. He is your Heavenly Father who delights in you and is the BEST matchmaker for your heart—

because He's the only one who truly knows every part. Now, being married for 33 years, I know that I could've never known all that my heart needed, but God did. I encourage you to trust Him too with your heart and with your husband-to-be. He is trustworthy. *"Trust in the LORD with all your heart, and lean not on your own understanding; In all your ways acknowledge Him, and He shall direct your paths." (Proverbs 3:5-6 NKJV)*

From Chelona Mama's heart...

The truth is, we can point you to all of these good practices, but at the end of the day, the choice is up to you. We hope you will listen to that little, quiet voice of the Holy Spirit. It's the voice that speaks to your heart and looks out for you. We hope through these pages you will feel exactly how much we are looking out for you. We want to do our best to protect you from anything that could cause heartache in the future.

We know that dating can be very exciting but also very complicated. In our current culture, there is such a heavy emphasis on sex appeal but giving into that mindset will most likely not produce your desired results. Sex appeal leads to lust, not love, and there is a big difference between the two. Overflow of butt cheeks and cleavage sends a clear message that you are NOT the woman MOYD will want to take home to meet Mom. He may want to take you home though, and that's "non buono—capisce?"

All jokes aside, the truth is you are worth so much more than you realize. We hope you know that God designed your body to be a gift to your husband. Your sexuality is a rare gem in the treasure chest of love.

Please pray the following prayer.

Dear Jesus,

Forgive me for any moments in my life
where I have made some poor decisions.
Help me to be honest with myself
to make the changes that are needed in
my life. Help me to understand that you
have great plans for me and MOYD,
whoever he may be.
Help me to be patient and trust You.
Most of all, help me to implement
Romans 12 :1
"...to offer my body as a living sacrifice,
holy and pleasing to You [God]..."
In Jesus' name,
Amen

Chapter 6

Social Media and Narcissistic Behavior

"Do not think of yourself more highly than you ought,
but rather think of yourself with sober judgment, in
accordance with the faith God
has distributed to each of you."
Romans 12:3

With the onset of social media in the early 2000s, we have noticed an increase in self-centered behaviors. Let's face it, it's fun to pose for a selfie every now and then, right? It's not wrong to post a selfie but there are healthy and unhealthy reasons to do so. Ask yourself, *"Why am I posting a selfie? Is it simply for fun? Is it to feel validated, valued, and celebrated? Will I be devastated if that certain someone doesn't like or comment on my post?"* What is the motivation or need inside of our hearts and minds that causes us to feel this need to share with the world everywhere we are going, everything we are doing, right down to pictures of things we are eating? Again, there are good reasons to share, but we must be honest with ourselves about our motivations and expectations.

We have become a culture that is less concerned about others and more concerned about ourselves. The constant need to impress our friends is a nagging voice in our heads. It seems that we are under the misconception that the best way to appease it, is to post yet another self-glorifying moment! But Philippians 2:3–4 encourages us to *"Do nothing out of selfish ambition or vain conceit. Rather, in humility value others above yourselves, not looking to your own interests but each of you to the interests of the others."*

As wives and mothers, Lona and I post a lot of pictures and updates, mostly of people we love because we know that life is fleeting! Basically, you blink and all of a sudden that precious little baby you were holding in your arms yesterday is off to college today. One of the greatest things about social media is when memories pop up on your wall and remind you of all the beautiful blessings you have experienced in this life; the graduation, trip with friends, family vacations, maybe even an engagement—it's all so wonderful, isn't it?

James 4:14 says, *"Whereas you do not know what will happen tomorrow. For what is your life? It is even a vapor that appears for a little time and then vanishes away."*

James refers to life as a vapor, like a mist that just vanishes before our very eyes. So perhaps that's why so many of us feel compelled to make this photographic montage of all of our greatest achievements and successes. Or maybe we just want to capture any sweet moment we are fortunate enough to experience this side of heaven. After all, life can be hard. That engagement photo or view of the Grand Canyon is a moment to treasure. Let's capture every moment we possibly can. In a world of uncertainty and pain, we find there are beautiful moments of hope to help us persevere through hard times and encourage others along the way. This is a healthy way to use social media, however, be aware that there are some pitfalls as well.

One of the biggest hazards of social media is the fact that once you post something, it is there forever. Your future could be affected by any post you put on the World Wide Web! Your family, future boyfriend, or boss may see these posts so be very careful what you put on the internet.

Another stumbling block of social media is the obsession it creates for us. It's like a really bad caffeine or sugar craving that you just can't do without! You find yourself convinced that you "need" to look at it again and again.

Research from GWI, Global Web Index, an audience research company reveals that "the 'typical' social media user now spends 2 hours and 23 minutes per day using social platforms. On average, that means that social media accounts for 35.8 percent of our daily online activities, meaning that more than 1 in 3 internet minutes can be attributed to social media platforms." Think of how much we could accomplish in that time instead of wasting it scrolling and posting!

If you are looking at the "like" or "heart" notification for gratification, you may be looking in the wrong place. If you are checking your social media every hour on the hour, you may be spending too much time focusing on things that really do not matter in the big scheme of life.

Many people struggle with feelings of anxiety or sadness after scrolling through social media. If you find yourself feeling sad or even depressed after viewing everyone else's happy montage, you may need to take a long break from social media altogether. Sadness or depression, thoughts of inadequacy, and feelings of hopelessness are indicators that there is something imbalanced in the way you are thinking about yourself. This is why we strongly suggest you take a break from social media for a little while and get into God's Word. His Word is powerful, and it can transform your life! Join a church, attend a singles event, call your friends, and make plans. Be around real, live people who bring you joy. Being around authentic people face-to-face is better than any social media influencer you will ever follow. Taking a break from social media is like a reset button for your mind. It will detox you from negative thoughts and reset the way you view yourself, others, and the world around you.

Questions to ask yourself about Social Media:

1. After spending some time scrolling through social media, how do you feel?

   _____

   _____

   _____

   _____

2. Are you constantly concerned about how many likes and comments you are receiving from your posts? If so, why?

   _____

   _____

   _____

   _____

3. When you post on social media, is it adding fulfillment and happiness to your life? Please explain.

   _____

   _____

   _____

   _____

4. Are you currently a professional influencer or hoping to become one? _____ What is your motivation and what is the purpose of your influence?

_____

_____

_____

_____

5. God wants to be our motivator in all that we do. If being rich and famous is your only motivating force, we suggest taking a break and seeking God for direction. Is being rich and famous your only reason to become a professional influencer on social media?

_____

_____

_____

_____

6. Are you aware that every time you post, you are actually influencing someone whether you label yourself as one or not? _____ Do you agree or disagree with this statement and why?

_____

_____

_____

_____

7. Please circle the items below that best describe your mental state after you spend hours on social media. Some of these points were inspired by a post from instagram.com/NeuroticMom.

    Ask yourself, "*Am I:*"
    - Feeling left out (FOMO—fear of missing out)
    - Sad and mentally exhausted
    - Mad at friends not responding
    - Feeling lonely
    - Questioning my purpose on social media
    - Depressed and struggling with suicidal thoughts

- Mentally exhausted but still functioning
- Discouraged but hopeful things will get better
- Relatively content and not affected at all
- Seeing some positive things and some negative
- Enjoying both viewing and sharing on social media
- Believing my posts are making a difference in the world
- Excited about what the future holds for me as an influencer
- Totally confident that I am right where I should be mentally
- Feeling like social media has no negative effects on me whatsoever

If your answers show that you are more negatively affected, do you think that it would be a good idea to take some time off of social media? If it is negatively affecting you, we want to encourage you to take a break because we truly care about your mental health and happiness.

We all need to be very careful who and what we allow to influence us. Reality dating TV shows are another example of something that can also have a negative effect on your life. We understand these shows display some of the most beautiful, romantic dates and the journey is always so amazing. As hopeless romantics, we can see the appeal of it all. While some contestants actually do find what they "think" is true love, others get their hearts trampled in the stampede during the competition and find themselves worse off than when they started. These shows encourage an impractical form of dating.

Matthew Keyser, a former reporter for the Daily Titan said, *"Many of these shows encourage an unrealistic view on compatibility and establishing a dream relationship by creating a gaming format that tests the boundaries of its contestants. Although these shows have entertainment value, they perpetuate a skewed version of love by promoting superficiality and toxic behavior."* We couldn't agree more with that statement.

Another negative factor we have noticed about these reality dating TV shows is the narcissistic element of it all. The bachelor gets to choose from a batch of "contestants" competing for his love. He can choose based on whatever he prefers or whoever he wants like he's shopping at the mall or walking into a candy store! These contestants will do anything to win the game. Some of these ladies are forfeiting who they really are in order to gain the bachelor's heart! But here is the harsh reality. Falling in love does not work this way. True love is not a game or a contest. When someone really loves you, they put your needs above their own, not the other way around. When two people are truly in love, all selfishness, self-centeredness, and narcissistic behavior need to vanish for the relationship to work.

Speaking of narcissistic behavior, when you are dreaming and planning to marry the man of your dreams, a narcissist will never be part of the plan. At first, you won't see him for who he really is because he hides *the ugly* so well. And it's easy to like a narcissist. They are usually charismatic, charming, thoughtful, and will act REALLY into you. You will easily be drawn to their magnetic personality while they mask an evil undercurrent lurking just below the surface. You will feel alive, happy, and safe when in their presence. They are interesting and mysterious. But their pride parading around as confidence is always present and comes out when they feel secure that they have you all to themselves to control and manipulate. Being married to a narcissist will be detrimental to every aspect of your life. A narcissist is never your MOYD. We've listed some warning signs to watch out for below.

Beware of anyone who:
1. spends the entire time bragging about himself and exaggerating his prowess
2. is full of vanity
3. doesn't ask you about your life and the focus is always on *numero uno*, himself
4. loves to talk about everything happening in his life, but doesn't seem interested in anyone else's accomplishments
5. puts you or others down in public
6. always has a critical opinion of others
7. is always the victim and blames others for all of his problems and never owns up to his own faults
8. is charming at first, but then becomes manipulative—it is his way or the highway
9. is very controlling
10. has a sense of entitlement
11. cannot compromise

12. hard to please
13. jealous
14. lacks healthy boundaries
15. expects special treatment
16. is a bully
17. twists the truth; lies
18. craves power
19. is a drama king
20. requires excessive admiration, praise, and recognition
21. lacks empathy or does not show genuine concern for you
22. lacks forgiveness and keeps a grudge or offense
23. consistently focuses on fantasies of becoming rich and famous
24. wants to hang out with materialistic, shallow people
25. is prideful and arrogant

The Difference Between Confidence and Arrogance

Confidence is the belief that you have achieved a certain level of success in a certain area because you have worked hard. Confidence says, *"I may not be perfect at this task, but I feel secure in my capabilities and talents."* Confidence comes from who we are in Christ. The fact that Jesus died for us so that we can live eternally suggests that our lives have amazing value. In Psalm 139:14 the Bible says, *"You are fearfully and wonderfully made."* You are God's workmanship. You are also beloved (Col 3:12), beautiful (Ps. 149:4), chosen (Eph. 1:4), precious (Is. 43:4), gifted (2 Tim. 1:6), safe (I Jn. 5:18) and loved (1 John 4:10) to name just a few attributes of who you are in Christ. This identity does not boast. It is a silent understanding that you are capable. Confidence is always accompanied by humility.

Arrogance is the belief that you have achieved a certain level of success because you think your abilities are far superior to everyone else's abilities. Arrogance says, *"I am better than everyone with similar talents and I deserve more than anyone else because of how great I am."* Arrogance comes from a constant focus on self and achievements. It loves to brag. It is a loud perception of their own capabilities. Arrogance is always accompanied with pride.

The Bible contains many scriptures regarding pride. Proverbs 8:13 says, *"To fear the LORD is to hate evil; I hate pride and arrogance, evil behavior and perverse speech."* Proverbs 11:2 says, *"When pride comes, then comes disgrace, but with humility comes wisdom."* Proverbs 16:5 says, *"The LORD detests all the proud of heart."*

We all struggle with issues related to pride every now and then. This does not make us all narcissists, but it is worth mentioning how Jesus feels about pride and the consequences that it brings. This encourages all of us to make better choices about how we view ourselves and how we treat the people around us. God blesses humility and a heart to serve rather than being served. Your MOYD should be someone who walks in confidence, not arrogance.

From Lona...

I personally have witnessed and experienced family members and friends with husbands who became ex-husbands after years of narcissistic behavior. I remember how I felt around them. I remember how they treated their wives. I remember sighs and sorrow-filled faces, regret, depression, hopelessness, and desperation. I remember comforting tears and hours of conversation. As I look back knowing what I know now, I see a thread of *ugly* behavior in the little and big moments throughout the years.

You may hear the word narcissist often these days. There are varying levels of course, depending on the person. We cannot make such a broad stroke for anyone showing signs to call them a narcissist, but we also cannot deny that they are out there and we need to be cognizant of their warning signs. Nobody should be treated with such deviousness, nor should anyone ever be belittled, controlled, or manipulated by any person.

If you feel like you currently have a narcissist in your life or you think you may be prone to some narcissistic behaviors yourself, please seek counsel from a person you can trust; a family member, good friend, mentor, or church leader would be great options. *"Where there is no counsel, the people fall; But in the multitude of counselors there is safety."* *(Prov. 11:14 NKJV)*

Roadmap to Moyd

1. Do you think you have a narcissistic boyfriend in your life right now? If so, what are the warning signs that you're seeing?

_____

_____

_____

_____

2. What do you think you should do about this?

_____

_____

_____

_____

3. Do you see any narcissistic attributes in yourself? If so, list them here.

_____

_____

_____

_____

Remember, we all struggle with self-centeredness from time to time. It doesn't mean you label yourself as a narcissist. It may simply be a nudge to intentionally work on that area of your life with someone you trust. If your boyfriend has some narcissistic tendencies, you may be thinking, *"Well, then my boyfriend can change too!"* However, you can only change yourself—you can't change somebody else. He must be willing to make necessary changes for himself and continue applying those changes for a long time before you commit to dating him again.

4. If you do see some narcissistic tendencies in yourself, what do you think you should do about them?

_____

_____

_____

_____

_____

_____

_____

5. Do you believe that you are worthy of the man of your dreams who will treat you well in humility, service, adoration, forgiveness, and love to name a few?

_____

_____

_____

_____

_____

_____

_____

6. If yes/no, please explain why?

_____

_____

_____

_____

_____

_____

From Chelona Mama's Heart...

We realize this may seem like a heavy chapter but when you work on yourself and resist the temptation of getting involved in an unhealthy, toxic marriage, it will pay off in the end. The journey to finding your husband may be filled with surprises and a lot of twists and turns along the way but true love is worth the adventure. Every girl deserves a pure, untainted, genuine, Prince Charming kind of love filled with respect, protection, adoration, service, humility, care, kindness, forgiveness, thoughtfulness, and FUN!

MEET MOYD

Let's end this powerful chapter with some powerful prayer—and remember,

YOU ARE

BEAUTIFUL

CHOSEN

PRECIOUS

GIFTED

ADORED

LOVED

AND WORTHY

OF THE

MAN OF YOUR DREAMS!!!

Dear God,

Help me to know my
worth and identity in you.
Help me to see the warning signs of
selfishness and narcissism in any man that
I may think is "the one."
Help me to be honest with myself and see
clearly even when my heart is aching for
the opposite. Surround me with good
counsel—people that will not just tell me
what I want to hear, but what I need to
hear. I know you want nothing but the best
for me. Thank you for loving me so
thoroughly and completely.
I love you too!
In Jesus' name,
Amen!

Chapter 7

The Birds and the Bees

"How beautiful you are and how pleasing, my love, with your delights!... I belong to my beloved, and his desire is for me."
Song of Solomon 7:6-10

I know you're anxious to learn more about MOYD and trust us—we can't wait to talk about him! We promise we'll get to the chapter that discusses in great detail who MOYD really is. But first, let's have a chat over the "elephant in the room," the sometimes awkward, yet sensitive and complex topic—SEX!

Don't worry, we will *try* our best to keep it "cringe-free" and not pontificate beyond our scope of understanding regarding sex education or theology. We want to share our thoughts with you about the most beautiful, intimate thing God created between a man and a woman. Before you meet MOYD, we want to establish in your mind and heart what God says about sex and why it's so important to do things His way.

We encourage you to read this section with an open mind. It's totally cool if you are laughing, crying, or rolling your eyes all the way through this chapter. Despite what you may think about us, we didn't grow up wearing Gunne Sax dresses and chastity belts running through the fields of innocence like something straight out of an early 1900s "Little House on the Prairie" movie. On the contrary, we simply know the beauty of sex and the blessing that it brings. We also fully understand that sex outside of the covering of marriage has the potential to drastically affect your life in negative ways as well.

Will you please allow us to impart some of our wisdom regarding this delicate subject? Some parts of this chapter may not apply to you at all. Maybe this will simply be a reminder and confirm what you already believe. To some it may be offensive, to others, it may be exactly what you may be going through. Some points may be harder to hear than others. Please know, you are not alone, and we don't think less of you and are not judging you. We love you and want what is best for you. Keep your seat belt fastened, your hands and arms should be inside of the roller coaster at all times and hold onto the safety bar in front of you. This may be a bumpy ride. Caution: You may want to keep your legs crossed during the ride (wink, wink—LOL).

Ok girls, it is completely normal and natural to have sexual desires because God Himself created these feelings inside of us. He gave us these feelings as a gift so that we may experience love in powerful ways through marriage. It is, however, a huge mistake to embark on sexual relations outside of the covering and commitment of marriage. Here are some reasons why.

1. Sex is not to be entered into lightly. Sex is sacred.
2. Sex is a blessing and is meant for the covenant of marriage. Genesis 2:24 says, *"For this reason, a man shall leave his father and his mother, and be joined to his wife; and they shall become one flesh."*
3. Sex was invented by God Himself as a gift to a man and a woman. When you have sex with

someone, you both are becoming "one." This creates a powerful bond. When two people have sex, there is no other bond on earth that can compare to this act. God meant it to be a beautiful physical, emotional, mental, and spiritual act between a man and woman under the umbrella of marriage to display the ultimate bond of love that we as humans can experience.

4. It is not healthy to have a "friends with benefits" mantra. No friends should have that kind of benefit.

We use the metaphor of "umbrella" because let's face it: SEX is like a raging storm of emotions and passion. Would you walk outside into a raging storm without an "umbrella" or some sort of covering to keep you protected? Of course not. Aside from being drenched, you might even be swirled up into the air like that scene with the tornado in the Wizard of Oz! Once the dust settles, what do you have left? What kind of commitment is he willing to give to you? Was it just a "one and done?" **You** may be giving yourself away out of pure love and devotion to him, but chances are, **he** may not be on the same page. If you are *not* under the umbrella of marriage, sex is just sex—it's just fun for the moment, but when the fun ends, he could leave. Most women think with their hearts, but in some cases, men think with...*well*...other parts (wink, wink). If that's the case, our hearts break with yours. Under the umbrella or covenant of marriage, there is a commitment in place. It is a contract. When the storms of life come, and they will, you both will be committed to working it out together so that neither of you will be able to jump ship!

5. Sex was never meant to be and should never be used as a barometer for measuring love.
6. When you have sex with someone, you see that person in an entirely different light. It is like a veil has been over your eyes and suddenly, that veil is lifted.
7. When you are with the *right* person at the *right* time, sex is one of the most wonderful things you can feel in this entire world.
8. When you are with the *wrong* person at the *wrong* time, sex can distort the way you see yourself and the world around you.
9. There is nothing wrong, ancient, weird, or ridiculous with waiting until you are married.

Ok, hold on a minute!!! Don't unfasten your seatbelt yet. We can see you rolling your eyes right through the pages. We can already hear you laughing at this idea but why *not* wait? What's the rush? Here's why we think you should wait.

Sex is more than a physical act. It is also emotional, mental, and spiritual. It is way too heavy to carry before the appropriate time. Most young women are not ready to handle sex and all of the responsibilities it brings.

Let's discuss the **physical, emotional, mental, and spiritual consequences** of having sex before the proper time. We'll begin with the physical.

The Physical Consequences:

1. You might possibly contract a sexually transmitted disease. According to the World Health Organization, it states that *"STDs have a profound impact on health. If untreated, they can lead to serious consequences including neurological and cardiovascular disease, infertility, ectopic pregnancy, stillbirths, and increased risk of Human Immunodeficiency Virus (HIV)."*

2. You could get pregnant before you're actually ready to be a mother. Your life as you know it would drastically change because you would be responsible for another human being. Mercymultiplied.com is a great organization helping young women ages 13-32 break free from life controlling issues and situations, including anxiety, depression, sexual abuse, eating disorders, self-harm, addictions, sex trafficking, and unplanned pregnancies. These residential services are offered free-of-charge.

3. In today's world, we understand that abortion is an option. We don't believe that abortion is the answer. Contrary to what you may be thinking, we actually **do** believe in freedom of choice. The choice is when you decide to have sex. If sex results in a pregnancy, and you decide that you cannot care for the child, we recommend allowing the baby to be adopted. There are so many families who desire children and can't have them. Adoption is a beautiful option for you. Abortion may seem like a quick fix to a scary situation, but in the end, the regret will be with you all of your life. We don't want you to go through that. As of March 4th, 2024, an article on

the The National Institute of Health website (nih.gov) states that *"Abortion either medical or criminal [due to rape], has distinctive physical, social, and psychological side effects. Abortion is known as a main cause of maternal mortality, life-threatening complications such as hemorrhage, fever, and infection on one hand, and psychological disorders such as regret, guilt, smoking, alcoholism, self-destructive behaviors, and even suicide on the other. Depression, worrying about not being able to conceive again and abnormal eating behaviors were reported as dominant psychological consequences of abortion as well as decreased self-esteem, and nightmares."* If you have already had an abortion, there is no judgment. We love you and God loves you. Your sweet baby is with Jesus in Heaven. If you feel like you are experiencing any negative effects from this decision, please reach out to a professional Christian counselor who can help you heal.

The Emotional Consequences:

1. Sex creates deep emotional bonds between two people. Have you ever had necklaces get tangled in your jewelry box? Sometimes, it is nearly impossible to unravel. Just like these necklaces, unhealthy emotional bonds are extremely difficult to untangle.

2. Any sexual act can be easily mistaken for love. When this happens and the relationship fails, you could find yourself in devastating heartache. This could also lead to anxiety and depression which could have long-lasting effects on your life.

3. The sad reality is that he may not be the one for you. Because of the physical pleasure sexual acts bring, you could find yourself emotionally fantasizing over a life with that person due to the sexual bond you created. The mind begins to create a picture of a happily ever after type of life, but that may not be reality.

4. Your reputation could be affected which can cause shame and humiliation among your peers.

The Mental Consequences:

1. You can become inappropriately obsessed with this person.
2. This relationship could consume your thoughts in unhealthy ways.
3. If the feelings are not reciprocated, you will feel rejected and could become severely depressed.
4. Depression turns to oppression that can turn into suppression. It will literally hold you back from pursuing all of your dreams, interfere with your happiness, and stop you dead in your tracks from accomplishing all of the wonderful things God has planned for you.
5. Devastating heartache can cause suicidal thoughts.

We need to stop right here and ask you something really personal. Have you ever suffered such severe heartache to the point where you felt like you wanted to die? Maybe you find yourself in that dark place right now. Honey, we hope you can hear our tender voices right through the pages of this book. Please hear us when we say, no failed relationship, no man, no poor choice, no sexual encounter, no bad friendship, no screw-up, no unwanted pregnancy, no abortion, no rape, no abuse, no school failure, no job failure—nothing in this world is worth ending your life over. If you are hearing a voice telling you that you want to die, that is the voice of the enemy. We are drowning out that evil voice right now and we're screaming through these pages loud and clear...

"NO WEAPON FORMED AGAINST
YOU SHALL PROSPER"
IN JESUS MIGHTY NAME— AMEN!
Isaiah 54:17

Now say these words out loud "I am dearly loved, accepted, chosen, precious, beautiful, protected, complete, forgiven, adored, wanted, valued, celebrated, and treasured!"

We want you to grasp how wide, how long, how high, and how deep is the love of Christ for you. And to know this love surpasses anything you have ever known or comprehended in your life so that you may be filled to the measure of all the fullness of God. (Paraphrased from Ephesians 3:18-19)

If you suffer from constant suicidal thoughts, please reach out to a family member, friend, or health professional or dial the suicidal hotline 988.

The Spiritual consequences:
1. Sex is not only physical, emotional, and mental but it is spiritual as well. After sex, the emotional connection may be over, but the mental and spiritual connections remain. This is one of the reasons why it is so heart-wrenching and difficult to overcome.

2. When people forget the sacred commitment sex creates, it opens the door for the enemy of your soul to torment you through your thoughts. Even after you have repented and moved past your mistake, the enemy is relentless. He will continue to bring up the memories to try to make you feel guilt and shame. This is why we, as your personal Chelona Mamas, desperately want to warn you so you don't open that door to the enemy.

3. Paul writes to the church of Galatia in *Galatians 5:19-21 "The acts of the flesh are obvious: sexual immorality, impurity, and debauchery; idolatry and witchcraft; hatred, discord, jealousy,*

fits of rage, selfish ambition, dissensions, factions, and envy; drunkenness, orgies, and the like. I warn you, as I did before, that those who live like this will not inherit the kingdom of God."

4. Since God blatantly instructs us to refrain from sexual immorality for our own good, we would be in direct disobedience to Him if we continue in this sin. It's important to understand that if we do not feel the conviction of the Holy Spirit when we commit these sins, we need to examine our hearts and ask ourselves, are we truly living a Christ-centered life? If we do not repent, this could affect us eternally. God's words are strong regarding refraining from sexual immorality along with many other sins listed below. He knows how sin can harm us. Like a good father, he wants to protect us from harm and heartache.

5. When we look at this list, we feel convicted about the areas of our lives where we struggle as well, therefore, we are not judging you. Only Jesus can judge whether or not a person will inherit the kingdom of God (Heaven). We are simply encouraging you to examine your heart and life. None of us are immune to any of the sins listed in the Galatians scripture above. In Romans

3:23 it says, *"We ALL have sinned and come short of the glory of God."* It is a healthy practice to bring our sins to the Lord and ask Him to forgive us and help us to overcome them.

6. Everyone has made mistakes and we want to make sure that you know beyond a shadow of a doubt that God **can** and **will** forgive you. You are not defined by any mistakes you have made. When you ask Jesus to forgive you, he wipes the slate clean. He literally forgets the mistakes you have made.

7. *"You will again have compassion on us; you will tread our sins underfoot and hurl all our iniquities into the depths of the sea." (Micah 7:19 NIV)*

8. *"If we confess our sins, he is faithful and just and will forgive us our sins and purify us from all unrighteousness." (1 John 1:9 NIV)*

Key Scriptures regarding sexual immorality:

Hebrews 13:4 says, "Marriage should be honored by all, and the marriage bed kept pure, for God will judge the adulterer and all the sexually immoral."

1 Corinthians 6:18-20 says, "Flee from sexual immorality. All other sins a man commits are outside his body, but he who sins sexually sins against his own body. Do you not know that your body is a temple of the Holy Spirit, who is in you, whom you have received from God?"

Colossians 3:5 says, "Put to death, therefore, whatever belongs to your earthly nature: sexual immorality, impurity, lust, evil desires, and greed, which is idolatry."

1 Thessalonians 4:3-5 says, "It is God's will that you should be sanctified: that you should avoid sexual immorality; that each of you should learn to control your own body in a way that is holy and honorable, not in passionate lust like the pagans, who do not know God."

Matthew 7:6 says, "Do not give what is holy to the dogs; nor cast your pearls before swine, lest they trample them under their feet, and turn and tear you in pieces." To clarify, giving your body away is like throwing your most valuable treasure to the dogs and pigs.

As we have mentioned, sex is so much more than just a physical act. It affects you physically, emotionally, mentally, and spiritually—this is why it is so difficult to break off the relationship because this type of bond can not be severed easily. The anguish you are feeling is a result of the intense bond pre-marital sex brings. It will take turning away from your sin, forgiving yourself, and praying to God for Him to completely release you from any bonds that you created with this person.

Before we go any further, if it seems overwhelming for you to get out of this relationship—trust us, we know you can. It is more simple than you think. When you ask Jesus to forgive you, He truly does. That means He wipes the slate clean and He does not keep a record of the sins you've committed. Isn't it so amazing that God literally forgets our transgressions when we bring them to Him? He is truly a good Father. We have asked God to forgive us for various sins throughout our lives and we encourage you to do the same. He is not mad at you. You are HIS creation, He adores you. You are His precious daughter and nothing you've done will ever change that. Trust us, we know this is true. Every time He looks at you, He just marvels over you with pure delight!!!

"The Lord your God is with you, the Mighty Warrior who saves. He will take great delight in you; in his love, He will no longer rebuke you, but will rejoice over you with singing."
Zephaniah 3:17

Would you like to ask God to forgive you for any past mistakes right now and help you to be stronger in the area of purity in your life? There is power in prayer. Simply ask Jesus to release you from the bond that is holding your heart hostage and sincerely pray the following prayer.

Dear Jesus,
Forgive me for creating any inappropriate bonds through sexual immorality. I repent and turn away from this unholy bond I created with (write his name here) _____. I release this person into your hands today. I know you have a better plan for my life and I surrender my life to you, in Jesus' name—Amen

Roadmap to MOYD:

1. Does it seem like it is nearly impossible to save yourself for marriage? If yes, why do you feel this way?

   _____

   _____

   _____

2. Do you feel pressure from society or from your peers to have premarital sex?

   _____

   _____

   _____

3. Do you feel any sense of guilt and shame after having sex? If you do, please know that God loves you and will cradle your heart. He longs to be gracious to you and will show you compassion. (Isaiah 30:18 NIV)

   _____

   _____

   _____

4. Do you feel like you can't stop having premarital sex? Why do you feel this way?

_____

_____

_____

_____

_____

5. After reading this chapter, do you understand why having premarital sex is harmful to you? Share your thoughts here.

_____

_____

_____

_____

_____

6. Do you need to make any changes to how you think or act about premarital sex? Please list these changes here.

_____

_____

_____

_____

_____

The Birds and the Bees

Before you exit this roller coaster ride, here are some tips to help you avoid falling into the temptation of sexual immorality:

1. Choose to go out on group dates rather than being alone with a guy.
2. Don't put yourself in a precarious or vulnerable position—it is very difficult to get yourself out of a sticky situation.
3. Don't be alone at his house or your house.
4. Don't let a guy see anything a bathing suit covers.
5. Don't let a guy touch anything a bathing suit covers. Some think, "a little touchy-feely is fine" but just like baseball, one base leads to another. Before you know it, you've gone too far.
6. There is an old saying that our Grannies used to say and they were right! "Why would he buy the cow when he can get the milk for free?"
7. Protect your "hoo-ha, your who-z-whatsit, va-jay-jay, your flower—whatever you call it, protect it at all costs. Your body is beautiful and worthy of respect and honor, nothing less.

From Chelona Mama's heart:

Remember, God created us and designed sex for us to be enjoyed to its fullest. It is an intimate, beautiful act that creates a unique, strong, beautiful bond with the man who is meant to honor, love, and respect you til' death do you part. It is more than just lust, a good time, or an extracurricular "one-night stand." Sex is sacred, holy, intimate, pleasurable, and powerful. When it is experienced with your spouse who has committed his life to you, for better or for worse, in sickness and in health—It is the best, most awesome, and wonderfully connecting, intimate experience ever. Nothing can compare to this kind of bond. This is the kind of bond that God has ordained and carries His blessing with it.

Girls, we totally understand the magnitude of sexual temptation. If you have suffered in any way because of a sexual relationship you were involved in, just bring it to Jesus. We promise He will come in like a flood. He will repair every single broken piece of your heart. He will take these broken pieces like shards of glass and turn them into a beautiful mosaic work of art!

Someday, when you are married to MOYD, you both will have the most beautiful life you have built together. You will look back at this time with nothing but thankfulness and gratitude. You will know that Jesus spared you from a life with the wrong person. We know what it means to be treasured and cherished. You will too!

MEET MOYD

Please pray the following prayer.

Dear Jesus,

Help me to trust you and
truly believe that
You are for me and not against me.
Heal my brokenness, every single part.
I surrender my life to You and ask You
to be Lord over every area of my life.
Help me to see myself
the way you see me.
Help me to believe
that you delight in me.
Help me to trust that You really do
have me in the palm of Your hand.
In Jesus' name,
Amen

Chapter 8

Who is MOYD?

"Take delight in the LORD,
and he will give you the desires of your heart."
Psalm 37:4

Before we describe in great detail who MOYD is and isn't, how about the chapter on the birds and the bees? Well, we sure are happy it's behind us! But in typical Italian Mother fashion, we need to mention just a few more thoughts regarding physical intimacy with MOYD.

1. MOYD is the epitome of the PERFECT GENTLEMAN.
2. MOYD would never force himself on you nor would he ever force you to do anything you do not want to do!
3. MOYD would NEVER pressure you into having sex or performing sexual favors.

4. MOYD does NOT watch PORNOGRAPHY and neither should you!

5. MOYD has nothing on his phone or computer that he needs to hide from you.

6. At the appropriate time, and at the appropriate place, MOYD will be a great kisser and he will be very affectionate.

7. Kissing MOYD will be one of your favorite things to do in this life!!!

Phew! We made it through the conversation regarding physical intimacy! That wasn't so bad, was it? We understand that some of the points listed are not the popular choice but let's be really honest here. Ask yourself this question, *"If my way is contrary to the way of dating described in this book, how has that been working out for me?"* We guess that it has not worked out the way you hoped. That is the exact reason why you are holding this book in your hand right now! Remember, if there is something on this list that you do not agree with, simply ask the Holy Spirit to reveal His truth to you. The Holy Spirit is that still small voice that keeps us on the right path. We totally understand how difficult it may be for you to unravel this in your mind. We also know that the Holy Spirit is powerful and wants to help you understand. Remember, He wants to have a deep relationship with you and be Lord over your life—every single part of it.

We want to help you understand that we have written this book filled with heartfelt advice inspired by our true life experiences. We are two moms who care so much for your heart. We are doing our best to address every possible obstacle you may encounter on your journey to your one and only MOYD. Here are a few more characteristics we believe MOYD will possess.

8. MOYD is NOT perfect. Neither are we. 😊

9. MOYD will work through his mistakes and learn from them. If you really love MOYD, you will FORGIVE him. If you exhibit grace and mercy for him, that will hopefully inspire him to do the same for you. Grace is kindness and compassion. Mercy means forgiving whether or not he deserves it. If you can not extend grace and mercy toward MOYD now, you will have a hard time doing so in your marriage. This is an important principle to put into practice now while you are dating.

10. MOYD will make mistakes, but he will be mature enough to admit them. (Most of the time 😊. That's where all that grace and mercy comes in.)

11. MOYD is a fun guy who makes you laugh.

12. MOYD is transparent and authentic.

13. MOYD is strong where you are weak and you are strong where MOYD is weak. You will complement each other.

14. MOYD is a man of integrity—he keeps his word and does what he says he is going to do.

15. MOYD is confident but not arrogant.

16. MOYD would never have any reason whatsoever to hit you—a real man NEVER raises his hand to a woman.

17. If a man hits you, HE IS NOT MOYD! He is an abuser. Do not give him a second chance, he doesn't deserve one. Run as fast as you can and never look back. If you feel like you are in any danger, contact the police. You may need a restraining order.

18. MOYD is patient.

19. MOYD will take all the time necessary to earn your trust and love.

20. MOYD is romantic, he is NOT a player.

21. MOYD is not afraid to hold your hand in public.

22. MOYD would never flirt with other girls— not in front of you or behind your back!

23. MOYD will always see you when others do not.

24. MOYD will always treasure and value your heart.

25. MOYD will hold your hair when you're puking.

26. MOYD does not always have to have his way.

27. MOYD will try to consider your feelings before his own.

28. MOYD will listen to your cry and try to help you fix whatever is breaking your heart if you want him to.

29. Even when MOYD doesn't look his best, he will always look good to you.

30. MOYD comes in all sizes—he is the perfect size for you.

31. MOYD might be a man in uniform, or he might be a sweaty football player, but no matter what MOYD does for a living—his profession will be good for your life together.

32. MOYD is your knight in shining armor. He is your Superman.

33. MOYD does his best to practice the 9 fruits of the Spirit. *"But the fruit of the Spirit is love, joy, peace, forbearance, kindness, goodness, faithfulness, gentleness and self-control.*

34. *Against such things, there is no law."* Galatians *5:22-23 (NIV)*

35. MOYD is not selfish and puts others before himself.

36. MOYD has a servant's heart. He will serve you happily. He will take out the trash, change the lightbulb, or maybe he will even rub your feet!

37. MOYD will challenge you in healthy ways to inspire and encourage you.

38. MOYD builds you up. He won't tear you down, belittle, or shame you.

39. MOYD has a J.O.B. and is a hard worker. He has plans for the future.

40. MOYD has big dreams and never gives up.

41. MOYD may be frugal but he is not a cheapskate.

42. MOYD is a good steward of his income.

43. MOYD is willing to go to church and serve at church.

44. MOYD always puts God first and so should you.

45. MOYD brings his tithes (1/10 of his paycheck) and offerings to God's house and you should too. *"Bring the whole tithe into the storehouse, that there may be food in my house. Test me in this, says the Lord Almighty, and see if I will not throw open the floodgates of heaven and pour*

out so much blessing that there will not be room enough to store it." Malachi 3:10 (NIV)

46. MOYD can't wait for you to meet his friends and family.

47. MOYD will stick up for you in front of his family, friends, and in public.

48. MOYD is a mighty man of God with integrity and great morals.

49. MOYD makes it a habit to surround himself with strong men who have good morals, keep him accountable, and give good, Godly advice.

50. MOYD is not afraid of standing up for what is right, even if it makes him unpopular.

51. MOYD prays for you, himself, and the world around him.

52. When MOYD is scared, he seeks God first.

53. When MOYD is discouraged, he goes to God in prayer.

Roadmap to MOYD:

1. Have you ever met a man who encompasses all of the qualities listed above?

   _____

2. When you look at this list of the attributes of MOYD, do you think it is possible that this man really does exist? _____Why or why not?

   _____
   _____
   _____
   _____
   _____

3. We believe that a good way to find your MOYD is to participate in activities that interest you. For example, if you have a heart for the homeless community, sign up to help through a church outreach program or organization. If you like hiking, join a community hike. If you love to read, join a book club. If you're a musician, join a band. This way, you will already have something special you both can enjoy together. With this in mind, what events or activities might you join to

possibly meet your guy? Have you made a list of qualities you desire in a husband that are important to you?

_____

List those qualities here:

_____

_____

_____

_____

_____

_____

_____

_____

_____

_____

_____

_____

_____

_____

_____

_____

From Cherie:

When I was single, a friend of mine asked me to make a list of everything I wanted in a man. I thought she was crazy and laughed at her yet she insisted I do this silly task. Since I thought this activity was so ludicrous, I decided I would make her the most unattainable list that seemed absolutely impossible to find in any one man. I was very specific in what I wanted in a man. I described exactly what he would look like, the kind of faith he would have, and his hobbies to name a few. She then said, *"Ok, now let's put your list in this envelope, seal it, and pray for him every day. When you finally meet the one God has for you, we will see what qualities he has from this list. If anything is missing, we will pray that it is something you can live without."* I thought this whole process was ridiculous.

When I was done with the list, I felt sad because I looked at it and truly thought this man did not exist on planet Earth. I was so WRONG! I am happy to report the man I married had everything on my list and more! He is not perfect, but he is perfect for me. So now I am going to ask you, *"If you haven't already, will you please make a list?"*

Who is MOYD?

Have fun and ask for everything, even the attributes you may think are silly or too much to ask for, and then pray and see what God will do!

(Your name) _____ **'s List for the Man of My Dreams!**

Eye Color: _____

Hair Color: _____

Age: _____

Height: _____

Ethnicity:_____

Favorite food:_____

Favorite Hobbies:_____

_____

Personality traits:_____

_____

_____

Any other attributes that are really important to you:

_____

_____

_____

_____

137

From Lona...

You may think this is silly, but one of the requirements on my MOYD list was the act of opening the car door for me. When a man does this, it demonstrates many great qualities that I desire in a husband such as gentleman-like behavior, kindness, humility, and exhibiting a servant's heart. Jim was the first guy to do this simple, yet profound act.

From Cherie...

I am a hopeless romantic and one of my all-time favorite things to do is go to the movie theatre and watch romantic movies. I love movies like "Braveheart" and "First Knight" when the heroes dressed in all their armor come riding into the scene on a white horse and save the damsel in distress. I love all things to do with castles, horses, bows and arrows, and fairytale endings. I also love dramatic, romantic movies that leave you breathless to the very last scene. I remember the day I saw "Message in a Bottle" starring Kevin Costner. It was shortly after my high school sweetheart and I had called off our wedding after 10 years of dating. I was devastated and my heart was so incredibly crushed. I was feeling extremely hopeless about my future. I went to see

"Message in a Bottle" and after the movie was over and everyone had left the theatre, I sat alone in the darkness and wept. I remember saying to myself *"This is the kind of love I want for my life. This man's love for his wife was incomparable to anything I had ever experienced before. I don't know if I really believe this type of love exists for me."* I was incredibly sad.

I wish I could go back in time and whisper to myself in that theatre *"Cherie, everything is going to be better than you ever imagined!"* Not only did God heal my brokenness, but He also brought my own Kevin into my life, and ironically, he actually even looks a little bit like Kevin Costner! God wrote the love story of my dreams for me! My husband is exactly like a knight in shining armor. The only difference was that it was a Los Angeles Police uniform he was wearing back then! God brought me a real-life superhero and his love for me transformed my life.

MEET MOYD

From Chelona Mama's heart...

Remember, there is no such thing as the perfect man but we believe there is the perfect man for you. He may not have all of the qualities you listed right from the start, but we are all a work in progress. Don't be so quick to dismiss someone if they don't fulfill everything on your list, especially physical qualities. We both had envisioned what our husbands would be like but who we married was different than what we had initially thought. When you meet your MOYD, if he is missing any attributes from your list, don't worry, you will be ok with it. It's amazing how our hearts changed when we met the man of our dreams. I (Cherie) adamantly said I would NEVER marry a cop, and I ended up marrying a Los Angeles Police Officer from a special force known as the CRASH unit! Now I can honestly say, I sure do love a man in uniform!!! And I (Lona) thought I would marry a man with dark hair, green eyes, and olive skin. My husband has blonde hair, and blue eyes and is a fair-skinned German Scottish man! I'm still hoping to see him in a kilt. 😄

Who is MOYD?

Remember, marriage is not only about falling in love, getting married, and possibly starting a family. It is also about what the two of you will accomplish together for God's kingdom—how you will impact others and the world around you.

So girls, be open to what God has for you. You will be happily surprised. True love works together and grows together. True love knows how to overcome any obstacle that crosses your path.

MEET MOYD

While you are waiting—pray the following prayer.

Dear Jesus,

I pray for the man who is on my list. I don't know
his name, where he lives, or what he does for a
living, but I know that you know exactly who he is.
Please put a hedge of protection
around him to keep him safe.
Bless him with whatever he needs. Lord Jesus.
Please lead him straight to me so we can begin our
lives together as husband and wife.
Help me to prepare for this man
and teach me your ways so
I can be the woman of his dreams.
Let us serve each other well and live an
abundantly blessed life.
I pray that you will bless him right now with
whatever he needs.
If he needs courage, fill him up.
If he needs strength, fill him up.
If he needs wisdom, Lord please fill him to overflow.
In Jesus' mighty name we pray,
Amen

Chapter 9

Red Flags, Rejections & Blind Spots

From Cherie...

One of my all-time favorite Disney movies is *Pinocchio*. I love the story of redemption that is woven throughout this movie. *Pinocchio* desires to become a real person instead of a wooden toy. His personal fairy Godmother tells him that all he has to do to become a real boy is prove himself worthy by being a good boy. She even sends Pinocchio a little cricket named Jiminy who acts as his conscience to help him along the way. Throughout the movie, you will see Jiminy doing his absolute best to keep Pinocchio out of trouble. He goes above and beyond to do so, and even puts himself in harm's way to protect Pinocchio from his own mistakes!

The Holy Spirit is our own personal "Jiminy Cricket." There are many times throughout our life when the Holy Spirit speaks to us in that still small voice to try to lead us onto the right path. Sometimes He will send people who have gone before us to try to warn us from making the same mistakes they did. As I mentioned earlier in this book, I was involved in a very long-term relationship that did not work out. God sent people to speak into my life during that time and I did not listen. There were many warning signs that I was not on the correct path that would lead to MOYD, but I ignored my "Jiminy Cricket." As a result, I suffered the incredible heartache of rejection because I ignored the red flags and couldn't see beyond my blind spots.

One of the most painful aspects of dating is the disappointment you suffer when it doesn't work out. As I mentioned in the previous chapter, after dating my boyfriend for nearly a decade, we finally got engaged. With a wedding dress bought and thousands of dollars spent, we planned a huge wedding in Historic Newport, RI—home of the Vanderbilts' summer mansions. Three months before it happened, we broke up! I was devastated and became extremely hopeless. I often look back at those years with so much regret. I wish I had listened to the Holy Spirit's gentle leading, but the heart wants what it wants. There were so many red flags during those years of our relationship, and I did not heed the warnings. My mother quoted this scripture to me often during that time, *"Above all else, guard your heart, for everything you do flows from it."* Proverbs 4:23 (NIV) I did not heed her warning. As a result, my heart was crushed into a million pieces. I became severely depressed and struggled with suicidal thoughts.

Some of my friends also disregarded the red flags in their relationships. They actually did go through with the wedding, had children, and suddenly found themselves knee-deep in some messy divorces! I wouldn't wish this on anyone. They were absolutely devastated and are still trying to recover from their loss many years later.

From my experience, I understand how hard it is to abandon a relationship with someone you thought was the perfect man for you. It is incredibly painful. Spending a decade with the wrong person taught me some really hard lessons. My family and friends warned me many times that this was not the right relationship for me but I did not listen. This relationship was a blind spot for me because I was caught up in many moments of romantic bliss. Since I had so much time invested, I desperately wanted him to be the one. I couldn't see the forest through the trees. All of my dreams and visions for my future were wrapped up in this relationship that was clearly not meant to be. When we broke up, it felt like God had taken someone precious away from me and I was so mad at God. However, I was wrong to feel angry at God because it was my actions that placed me in the center of my heartache.

The next couple of years were laced with all kinds of relationship mistakes. My heart was broken, and I also broke some hearts along the way. During this season, I was working three different jobs just to stay afloat and one of my bosses made inappropriate advances towards me. I was in a vulnerable position and as a result, I let my guard down. He was a lot of fun to be around and I needed some laughter in my life. I started envisioning what a life with him would look like. In my mind, everything began to make sense as to why the other relationship did not work out. But the truth is, I began to develop true feelings for a man who did not have true feelings for me. He was not in love with me at all. He was not my MOYD and being with him was another relationship mistake. He took advantage of me during a time when I was incredibly vulnerable, and I was foolish to fall into such a trap. Even though office romances have become more acceptable in today's society, I would like to caution you to refrain from getting romantically involved with your co-workers, especially with someone who is in a leadership role over you. The relationship between an employer and employee needs to remain professional at all times. This can become a major blind spot and can cause you serious damage, not only emotionally, but also financially and professionally. While my relationship conundrum did not cause permanent damage, it definitely delayed my life in many ways, especially my healing process. I wasted precious time out of my life trying to overcome my heartache. My heart was wrapped up in a tangled ball of yarn and it took a lot of effort to get emotionally healthy again. Thankfully, God is such a gracious, compassionate God who cares for us deeply. He made Himself tangibly real to me during this time and transformed my life in amazing ways. God removed some harmful people and toxic situations from my life and replaced them with people who cherished and treasured me.

I had no idea that someday I would look back on that difficult season and actually thank God for not allowing those relationships to work out. Those rejections paved the way for me to get onto the right path that would eventually lead me to MOYD! Girls, you will never believe what happened next!

I was always the bridesmaid, and never the bride, and on one hot summer day in Newport, Rhode Island I served in my friend's wedding where I met the ultimate man of my dreams—Kevin Adams! I was a bridesmaid, and he was a groomsman. At one of those beautiful historic mansions overlooking the ocean, with my arm in his, we walked down the aisle together that day. We had no idea that on one hot summer day 11 months later, we would again, walk through that same beautiful mansion overlooking the ocean in Newport, Rhode Island as husband and wife! From that day forward, there was a major shift in my perspective. The most important lesson to learn from this story is that your story *can* change. When I thought I would never have a happy ending because of my past experiences, I began to feel hopeless about my future— I was completely wrong. Kevin and I have been happily married for over 23 years and we have three beautiful children. I never imagined my life would be so blessed!

I learned a very important lesson during that time in my life. The heartbreak I suffered did not happen *to* me, it happened *for* me—for my benefit so I would find the right person. When I was incredibly broken, Jesus became my everything. He healed me, made me whole, and led me straight to MOYD. This difficult journey made me appreciate Kevin so much more. My mother used to tell me the other guys did not treasure and cherish me and I never understood what she meant until I met Kevin.

Roadmap to MOYD:

1. Do you have some "Jiminy Crickets" in your life that can actually speak into your life and offer you sound, biblical advice for your situation? If so, write their names here:

_____

_____

_____

_____

2. Are you in a relationship right now that feels hopeless and full of despair? If yes, why does it feel this way?

_____

_____

_____

_____

3. If God were to tell you to lay this relationship down, would you be willing to really lay it at His feet and walk away?

_____

4. If you answered no, please explain why you feel like you cannot walk away from this relationship.

_____

_____

_____

_____

5. Sometimes it helps to be able to talk to someone when you are facing a hard decision. Would you be willing to seek Pastoral or professional Christian counseling regarding this?

_____

_____

_____

_____

6. Do you trust that God has His absolute best plan for your life?

_____

If you answered no, please explain here.

_____

_____

_____

_____

7. Sometimes we tend to hold onto things like a "dog with a bone." Are you willing to trust God completely and make the hard decisions about your future regarding MOYD, career, or anything else He asks you to lay down? If no, please explain.

_____

_____

_____

_____

_____

_____

_____

_____

_____

From Chelona Mama's heart...

Did you know that the Bible says in *Psalm 34:18* *"Jesus is near to the brokenhearted and he rescues those whose spirits are crushed?"* Isn't it amazing that Jesus, our precious Savior is right there in the midst of all of our pain? We know you can't physically see Him but we want to encourage you to have faith that His loving arms are wrapped tightly around you right now wherever you are!

If you are hurting from a recent breakup, we also want to encourage you to lean into Jesus. He is literally weeping when you weep and His heart hurts for you more than you can possibly understand. God can handle your hurt and your anger. If your heart is shattered like broken glass right now, we want you to know that we understand your grief! We have such a deep love of Christ for you. You matter to God, and you matter to us!

The first step in your healing process is to invite Jesus into your situation and ask Him to help you through this season of change. The second step in your healing process is to recognize that God is sovereign. Merriam-Webster Dictionary describes the definition of sovereign as *"one possessing or held to possess supreme political power; one that exercises supreme authority within a limited sphere; It often describes a person who has supreme power or authority, such as a king or queen*; power that cannot be checked by anyone or anything."

As followers of Christ, we are asked to rest in God's sovereignty. Sometimes it is really hard to accept when things don't go our way. At times, we are under the misconception that because we are daughters of the King, we get everything we want but that is not always the case.

This is when our trust in God's plan and keeping the faith while waiting collide. Our heavenly Father wants to give to us abundantly every single beautiful blessing that He has planned for us. Sometimes it takes longer than we want it to and that is difficult to navigate through. If you are in a long season of waiting for God to come through for you, We would like to remind you of a few things to keep close to your heart.

1. God is your best friend and you are never alone. *"The Lord is close to the brokenhearted and saves those who are crushed in spirit."* *Psalm 34:18 NIV*

2. When you find yourself in a swirling mega storm of life, you can always find shelter in Jesus. Psalm 91:4 NLT says, *"He will cover you with his feathers. He will shelter you with his wings. His faithful promises are your armor and protection."*

3. Deuteronomy 31:8 says," Do *not be afraid or discouraged, for the LORD will personally go ahead of you. He will be with you; he will neither fail you nor abandon you."*

4. God is always good, no matter what season of life you find yourself in.

5. Jeremiah 29:11 says, *"God has plans to prosper you, not to harm you, plans to give you hope and a future!"*

MEET MOYD

We hope you feel God's love, presence, and peace.
Please pray the following prayer.

Dear Jesus,

Help me to listen to the "Jiminy Crickets"
you have placed in my life.
Give me the strength to walk away from a relationship
if it is not the man you want me to be with.
Lord, help me to trust you completely
with my whole heart.
I hold onto Your promises that
You have plans to prosper me and give me a future.
You have the best plan for my life
already mapped out.
I cried until my eyes ran dry and
You were there through it all.
I know that you will never leave me or forsake me.
You are the Alpha & Omega,
the beginning, and the end.
You know how to write my love story
better than I ever could...
So Lord, I am handing the pen over to you this day.
Do what You want to do in my life.
In Jesus' name,
Amen

MEET MOYD

Chapter 10

Before You Say, "I Do!"

"Be of one mind, united in thought and purpose." I Corinthians 1:10b

From Lona...

I wish I knew then, what I know now. Jim and I were babies when we married. I was barely 19 and Jim was 21. I had just graduated from high school and girls—it was a whirlwind. We met in October, got engaged in December, and married in July. We didn't really have time to discuss much of anything other than, "What color is your tux?" and "Where will our honeymoon be?"—LOL. I do remember talking about how many children we wanted. We agreed on four and ended up having two because our daughter Kayla came sooner than expected. Brendan was only six months old when I became pregnant with our Diddly Doo. It was almost like having twins. We wouldn't change a thing, but in the moment we decided, we were done.

Being so young, Jim and I basically grew up together into adulthood and figured out life as we walked through it. We met at church, which I highly recommend. This set the stage for a strong foundation that helped us make many heavy decisions lighter. But even with the same faith, we were still two individuals with different thoughts and ideas. Thankfully, we both have pretty chill personalities. Well, Jim is more laid back than I am. 😎 For the most part, we have interacted with each other amicably, but if we'd asked some of the "BIG" questions before we said, "I do!" a few chapters in our marriage would have gone a lot smoother with expectations more clearly aligned. Much hurt, resentment, and heartache could have been avoided. For example, when one person expects to live in the heart of the city and the other wants to live in the suburbs, this can be an area of resentment or contention in the future. Marriage can be blissful and beautiful, but it can also be challenging and difficult at times. This is why I recommend being an open book with each other before walking down the aisle. Talk honestly about your hopes, dreams, plans, and expectations to help create the happily ever after that you desire.

One area that I wish Jim and I had discussed in more detail before marriage was regarding finances. According to a *Money Magazine* poll, 70% of married couples argue about money more than household chores, time spent together, sex, snoring, and what's for dinner. According to the *National Institute of Health*, 37% of all divorces in the United States occur as a result of financial problems. These are sobering statistics.

I'll never forget the conversation I had with my sweet dad in the car on the morning of my wedding day. After he drove me to get my hair styled and my veil in place, He said, *"Honey, communication is the key to marriage. It doesn't matter what the subject matter is, but always keep an open line of communication and keep communicating no matter what."* My parents have now been married for over 58 years. I think he was onto something.

Healthy communication involves two people sharing information in an amicable manner whereby each person listens to understand, not just to be understood. If there is a disagreement, there may need to be a compromise to come to a resolution both individuals feel good about. Jim and I were busy young adults with full-time jobs. I was involved in worship, women's, and childcare ministries. Jim was involved in baseball, basketball, and softball leagues. With holidays, and family and friend engagements, communication was often last on the list or lost in translation. This resulted from miscommunication, not enough communication, or the lack of it. And if I'm being completely honest, sometimes I really did not want to communicate at all. I was hiding behind a mask of excuses.

Whether the issue was not telling each other about spending money on items we didn't really need or have the money for, loaning money, hiding a "cash stash" or insufficient funds fees—the struggle, frustration, hurt, guilt, shame, and resentment was real. As we swept each conversation under the rug, a thick brick wall began to be built where a bridge used to reside. This began a domino effect of disconnection. Conversations were strained and became shorter and shorter. Isolation started creeping into our marriage which negatively affected every area of our relationship.

There is a freedom in honesty. When Jim and I finally really connected and communicated about everything, even if it was a difficult subject to talk about, we always felt better in the end. We loved each other enough to work through the difficulty and stand on solid common ground. We forgave and gave grace knowing we were a work in progress and our love was worth the work. We made some necessary changes and set up new strategies to not end up in the same place twice. Did we mess up again and again— absolutely. But, that is when forgiveness meets grace and keeps flowing. We have been happily married for over 33 years.

If you'd like to skip a few fights, tears, frustration, isolation, and heartache—keep reading girls. Planning your future together can be a very fun and romantic activity to do. It's a twinkling of fairy dust feeling when you dream together. Prince Charming has met Cinderella and now they are planning for the wedding, honeymoon, and how they are going to run their kingdom. Cherie and I, as your Fairy Godmothers are waving our wands, and glitter is swirling around everywhere...Ah— what bliss! But I'm sure even Prince Charming and Cinderella disagreed on a few things that had to be worked out along the way.

165

Listed below are a series of questions that we believe to be hot topics during marriage and are very important to discuss *before* you say "yes" to the dress. Choose a private place with a relaxed atmosphere to talk where you both feel at ease. You don't want to be anywhere that you can be interrupted. No Dave and Buster's, ok?—LOL! This list is not meant to be exhaustive and please add or alter as you see the need for your particular situation. These subjects can become areas of disagreement if your expectations don't match. If this happens, you will need to talk through your differences and try to come up with a compromise that you both feel good about. You may be shocked with how strongly he disagrees in any given area. This is good. It helps you understand what is important to both of you, what you can work through, or what might be a deal breaker. Listen with an open mind and humble heart. Don't talk over each other, or become impatient. Trust the process. It will be worth it. Having this discussion gives each other the time and space to process. This is the next big step and hopefully the final step before pre-marital counseling and picking out what china you would like to use when the family visits for Thanksgiving. This step is crucial to do before marriage. An outside voice is necessary to ask questions that you may not have considered.

Treat yourself! After you go over the questions, do something fun or go to your favorite place together. This may sound unnecessary, but it gives you something to look forward to and will lighten the mood, especially if you've had to work through some areas of disagreement. Remember, a disagreement does not mean you are incompatible. You may just need to spend extra time to work out your differences.

OK—here are some topics to discuss. Again, please add or alter the questions according to what is important to both of you. Be honest, DREAM BIG and have FUN! You are planning the future of your happily ever after together (cue the fairy dust)!

1. We all have different expectations of how our married life will look. What kind of lifestyle do you expect to have, a modest one or a life of luxury?

    _____

    _____

    _____

    _____

2. What kind of home would you both like? What size, style, how many bedrooms, etc.? Do you need a man cave, a craft room, a studio, or a garage? What are your deal breakers (the options you can't live without)?

    _____

    _____

    _____

    _____

3. Where would you both like to live? In the heart of the city, in the suburbs, or in a rural area?

    _____

    _____

    _____

    _____

4. Where would you like to travel and what are your dream vacations?

_____

_____

_____

_____

5. What kind of ministry or outreach would you like to serve in?

_____

_____

_____

_____

6. What charities would you like to support?

_____

_____

_____

_____

7. What are your hobbies?

   _____

   _____

   _____

   _____

8. Will you both work? Part-time/Full-time? Outside
   of the home or remotely?

   _____

   _____

   _____

   _____

9. Do you both want to have children? If not, please
   give a brief explanation.

   _____

   _____

   _____

   _____

10. If yes, how many children would you like to
    have? _____

11. Are you both open to adopting children?

_____

Why or why not?

_____

_____

_____

_____

12. If you have children, will you both be working part-time or full-time? preschool? _____

K-8 _____ 9-12 _____

13. If you don't have the same faith/religion, will one person convert? How will you navigate those religious differences? Just two cents from your Fairy Godmothers—*we **highly recommend marrying someone <u>within</u> your faith.*** Not doing so will complicate things, especially on holidays with in-laws and if you have children. Your faith filters through everything you do. This decision will affect every aspect of your entire life together.

_____

_____

_____

MEET MOYD

14. Are you going to attend church? If so, which
church will you attend—his, yours, or a new one
you choose together?

_____

_____

_____

_____

15. Will you tithe? A tithe means one-tenth in
Hebrew. Christians give one-tenth of their
income to support their local church which
supports ministries to help people in time of need
and to share the gospel locally and around the
world. Malachi 3:10 says, *"Bring the whole tithe
into the storehouse, that there may be food in my
house. Test me in this," says the* LORD *Almighty,
"and see if I will not throw open the floodgates of
heaven and pour out so much blessing that there
will not be room enough to store it."* God has
continually blessed our families over the years
as we have given to our local church. It's a really
great feeling to be a part of helping others
literally all over the globe.

_____

_____

16. Will you each have separate bank accounts or one joint account together? Once again, your Fairy Godmothers are here. We want to encourage you to make sure you both have access to all accounts. Nothing should be hidden from each other, especially money.

_____

_____

17. How much debt do you have together? What is your plan to pay it off? If you need a strategy for your debt, refer to the book *Financial Peace Revisited* by Dave Ramsey.

_____

_____

_____

_____

18. Where do you see yourself in 5, 10 & 15 years?

_____

_____

_____

_____

_____

From Lona...

YOU DID IT! Phew—Girl, I know that must've taken a lot of energy and I am so proud that you and your MOYD took the brave step to answer some BIG questions. I hope you had fun! Don't worry if the conversation ended up being a hot mess at times. Beginning the conversation is the important part. There are no right or wrong answers and no one is receiving a high or low score. I know you may be thinking, *"My answer is the correct one—LOL!"* But the correct answer is when you both agree.

A healthy relationship is finding common ground that sometimes requires sacrifice and compromise. This discussion will tell a lot about your relationship. As long as you are both willing to work things out, you'll be just fine. Through the years, wants and needs change, but having this conversation ahead of time sets a strong foundation to build upon and saves you from arguments in the future and maybe even divorce. If you can't agree on a specific subject, don't force the issue. Give each other time and space to process. You can circle back when you both are ready. And sometimes, you can simply agree to disagree.

Roadmap to MOYD:

1. What question brought you both the most joy, giddiness, or laughter and why?

   _____

   _____

   _____

   _____

   _____

2. Was there a question when MOYD'S answer surprised you?

   _____

   _____

   Was it a happy or sad surprise?

   _____

   _____

   Explain why you were surprised.

   _____

   _____

   _____

   _____

3. Was MOYD surprised by any of your answers?

_____

_____

Was it a happy or sad surprise?

_____

_____

4. Ask him to explain why he was surprised.

_____

_____

_____

_____

5. What question was the most difficult to discuss?

_____

_____

_____

_____

Why was it difficult?

_____

_____

_____

_____

6. Were you able to work through the difficult question or did you agree to disagree? Please explain.

_____

_____

_____

_____

_____

_____

_____

_____

_____

_____

_____

_____

_____

_____

_____

_____

From Cherie...

When I look back on my life, I do have some regrets. I wish I wasn't so deeply involved in such a serious relationship so young. I could've gone straight to New York or Los Angeles right after high school and pursued my deepest passions in singing and acting. Unfortunately, fear of the unknown crippled me. I was afraid to leave what was comfortable. If I did not let my fears control my decisions, who knows? I may have met Kevin sooner! Nevertheless, God took care of me. He gave me a wonderful career—I recorded albums and toured all over the world.

Thankfully, I eventually met Kevin even though it was later in life, and we now have 3 beautiful children. God has a plan for our lives, but He also gives us free will. Our choices always influence the outcome of our lives. This is why I have found it imperative to seek God through every twist and turn of life. *Colossians 3:15 (KJV) says "Let the peace of God rule your heart..."* and I have learned to be sure to have that peace before I make any big decisions especially when it has to do with who you will marry.

When you become married, the two of you together have to find that same peace in the decisions you will make for your family.

MEET MOYD

Please pray the following prayer.

Dear God,

Help me and _____ (insert
Moyd's name;) find your peace as we
discuss what is important to both of
us for our future life together. Help
us to listen with an open mind and
humble heart. If we disagree, help
us find common ground that we both
feel good about. Help both of us to
create an atmosphere for each other
to feel heard, loved, valued,
understood, and seen.
And then we can kiss about it ;)
In Jesus' name,
Amen.

Chapter 11

Butterflies, Fireworks and Rainbows

"He that dwelleth in the secret place of the most High
shall abide under the shadow of the Almighty
I will say of the Lord, He is my refuge and my fortress:
my God; in him will I trust."

Psalm 91:1-2

From Cherie...

When I was a little girl, I was obsessed with rainbows and butterflies, especially the black and yellow striped ones. Just down the street from my house was a meadow that led to the woods. I used to go to that meadow often with my net and would pray that one of those unique striped butterflies would flutter my way. Before I went butterfly hunting, my mom would say *"Cherie, make sure you don't go too far. I don't want you getting lost in those woods!"* Most of the time, my net would remain empty but every once in a while, God would surprise me with really stunning butterflies. I would do my best to catch it but to no avail, that stripey fellow would just float on by. Despite my mother's warning, there were times when I would chase it deeper into the meadow, towards the woods.

The feeling of falling in love is often compared to the flutter of butterflies in your stomach, an explosion of fireworks when you kiss, and when things are going really well, falling in love is like seeing rainbows of pure bliss. These experiences are lovely in all of their glory however it is very easy to get lost in them! Be careful, it is possible to feel these things with any guy. It doesn't necessarily mean he is the one. Those fun, exciting feelings can change with the wind. Feelings can also lead you astray if you are not careful. This is why we don't base our decisions to marry someone based on these types of physical feelings. Rather, we encourage you to listen to your Jiminy Cricket (Holy Spirit) and live a life fully surrendered to Jesus. I have learned that those wonderful feelings are to be enjoyed, but they are not meant to lead you into your destiny. I promise you will experience all of those things and more when you meet MOYD!

Butterflies and fireworks are indicators that the relationship is indeed enjoyable but only the peace that God brings can determine who you should marry. *"Now may the Lord of peace himself give you peace at all times in every way. The Lord be with all of you."* *2 Thessalonians 3:16 NIV*

There were a couple of guys in my single years who I thought were wonderful in every way. They took me on some really fun dates and were complete gentlemen. Every time I was with them, they made me feel special. But there were moments when I just knew they were not right for me. There wasn't any good, solid, or specific reason necessarily. I couldn't explain why—I just knew that they were not my MOYD. When I met Kevin, he was living on the West Coast and I lived in Nashville. Having a life together looked impossible, but for some reason, I felt the peace of God when I was with him. The "fireworks" between us were nothing short of AWESOME, but it was the peace that I felt in my heart that made me realize, *"Kevin is my MOYD."*

Times with MOYD will feel like fireworks on the fourth of July but remember, there will also be times when life sends you curve balls. If you are dating a guy based on all of the fluttery things, what happens when real life begins and you find yourself struggling to find those butterflies you once felt? Those are the moments when you must lean into Jesus together. This is why you and MOYD need to be on the same page spiritually. You will always have some differences between you but at the end of the day, you both will be able to work it out together with Jesus at the center of your relationship.

From Lona...

Have you ever experienced a moment during your relationship with MOYD when you felt *forever*? This moment is like no other moment. It is a "butterflies, fireworks, and rainbows" kind of moment—the turning point of your relationship when you feel deep in your gut, *"This is the one!"*

During the very short time that Jim and I dated, we served in the AWANA teen ministry at our church. This "forever" moment happened during a winter weekend campout for the teens. The entire weekend was like a dream. It was a perfect winter wonderland in Upstate NY where the snow was crunchy which made for excellent packing for our playful snowball fight. The nightly bonfires brought cozy warmth and closeness as we made smores together, sang songs, and shared stories of God's love with the teens. We also went horseback riding *(what girl doesn't like a romantic horseback ride in a wintery wonderland Narnia of romantic bliss?)* and watched our first movie together, *Field of Dreams*. It was all very dreamy...

One of the craft activities was to make a leather belt. There were iron stamps that punched letters and designs into the leather. Did I necessarily want to make a leather belt? Not really, but I didn't care what Jim and I were doing as long as it was together. I can't remember what my belt looked like, but I remember Jim's belt and still have it to this day. I'll never forget his sweet proud smile when he gave it to me. Stamped into the leather were his initials J.E.F (James Edward Fraser), then three hearts with a large one in the center, then my initials L.R.S. (Lona Renée Fraser). As I read the design from left to right, my heart started to pound out of my chest. And over and over, all I could hear in my heart was *"Jim loves Lona! Jim loves Lona! Jim loves Lona!"* Well girls—let me tell you, that was it! The moment when my heart melted for this meek, kind, generous, sweet, servant-hearted gentleman who at this point had opened the car door for me many times.

As I'm typing these words, the memory still brings me to tears. This was the man I was going to marry. This was the man of my dreams. The kind of man that would love me the way a man is supposed to love a woman. A gentleman who would care for my heart with kindness, strength, humility, generosity, and forgiveness. He would laugh, cry, snuggle, play, hug and kiss me. He would provide, nurture, fix the sink, take out the garbage, ride a rollercoaster, travel, and share his dreams with me. I was done looking and praying. I could trust this man with my whole heart and I felt at peace. This is when I felt forever.

Roadmap to Moyd:

1. Have you felt fireworks or seen butterflies or rainbows with your boyfriend? If so please explain the moments.

   _____

   _____

   _____

   _____

2. Do you feel at peace when you are with your boyfriend? Please explain when you felt this.

   _____

   _____

   _____

   _____

3. Have you felt a "forever" moment with your boyfriend? Please explain.

   _____

   _____

   _____

   _____

From Chelona Mama's Heart...

When we look back over the years, we realize that life has taken us on quite the journey. While some roads led to regret, other roads took us to places of pure bliss and blessings beyond our imagination. God continues to surprise us with things that we never imagined were possible. Through every twist and turn, we realize that God had His hand on us the whole way through.

We are praying for you and we are believing with you that as you surrender every single part of your life, God will be preparing the perfect mate for you. It has been our honor to walk alongside you in your journey to your MOYD. We hope our advice guided and challenged you and gave you strategy, healthy boundaries, confidence, and hope.

The journey to finding MOYD is such an exciting time. Please continue to use this book to reference, review, and refresh along the way. Please share your stories and pictures at chelonashow@gmail.com. We would love to hear from you! We are also developing a new show called "The Chelona Show." You can follow us on Instagram @Chelonashow.

Of course, we will end in prayer. We love each and every one of you.

Dear God,

Thank you for butterflies,
fireworks, and rainbows,
but most of all for caring for
and protecting my heart.
Thank you for loving me
the way that You do.
I love you too.
Help me to continue to guard my heart
to keep me from harm and heartache
and trust You as
You lead and guide me
to find the man of my dreams.
Help me to be
the woman of his dreams as well and
help us to love and serve you
all the days of our lives.
I know You want to bless us and that
You have great plans for us.
In Jesus'
Amen

Love's Eloquence

Speak to me

Not with words I can hear

But can feel

Not with the tone of your voice

But the touch of your soul

Reaching out to mine

With the embrace of Romeo

And the response of Juliet

No words express as much as

The connection between your heart and mine

This is love's eloquence

That has no clock, no boundaries of location

No recognition of time

Lona Renée Fraser

♥ *Thank*  *You* ♥

We laugh all the time about where *MEET MOYD* began and where it ended. We laughed, we cried, and had some really challenging discussions. This journey has made us stronger, wiser, and even more compassionate for the singles scene.

We are ever so thankful for our families, friends, and the many mentors who through the years have shared their love, experience, and wisdom with us and helped us in our own journeys. The wisdom we gained is all throughout these pages.

To all of our readers—YOU ARE AWESOME! We love you and will continue to pray for you. Never give up and never settle for less than the man of your dreams!

Most importantly, we are so thankful to God our Heavenly Father and Savior Jesus Christ for loving us girls so sacrificially and unconditionally. We would never be the wives, moms, daughters, sisters, or friends we are without the abundant love you first showed us. We love you!

From Lona: ♥

Thank you to my husband **Jim** who gave up many date nights as I wrote this book and never complained about my absence. As always, you are my silent strength. It was fun writing about how I prayed for you, what it meant for you to open my car door for me, and how I felt when I knew you were "the one"—the man of my dreams. I love you Jimmers.

Mom and Dad, I would not be the woman I am today without you. You taught me compassion, integrity, and a hard work ethic as I witnessed yours. Mom, your smile taught me to smile. Dad, your strength made me strong. And Dad, I am a storyteller and teacher because I learned from the finest—you.

Mom and Dad Fraser, Thank you for your prayers and for raising such a wonderful man.

Bro! You are a superhero of perseverance, loyalty, and compassion and you've helped instill these characteristics in me as you have exemplified them in your own life, except of course when we were little and we drove each other crazy as all good siblings do;)

To my **BFF Debi, aka Dab.** Thank you for your prayers, encouragement, love, laughter, and support! You have been an inspiration in my life for over 20 years now and I don't know what I would do without you.

To **Heartprint Writers' Group,** thank you for your prayers, encouragement, and support! It means the world to me. You are my tribe.

What can I say **Cherie**—WE DID IT!!! Girrllll, thank you for asking me to be a part of your vision, for your boldness in Christ, and for working so hard. Your tender heart for single women inspires me. The care and love you have shown, the prayers you have cried, and every chapter that is written in this book is an outpouring of your heart to single women. We will never know the impact this book will have on this side of Heaven. I am so thankful, grateful, and humbled that you trusted me with your vision
—Wonder Woman powers unite!

Thank *You*

From Cherie:

Ron and Cheryl Paliotta, for setting an excellent example of what a Godly marriage looks like. Mom, you taught me that if I put Jesus first and made Him my everything, all good things would be added to my life. After my first heartbreak, I thought I would never love again—you assured me that I would. I was wrong, you were right. Thank you for teaching me how to be a good wife and mother. Dad, you set the bar so high, I wasn't sure I would ever be able to find a man as good as you! The way you love and care for Mom is a beautiful thing. You have worked hard your entire life making beautiful jewelry and we felt like princesses adorning ourselves with it! (www.musicandheartjewelry.com)

Ron and Lori Termale, thank you for loving my kids so well, even across the miles! Lori, you are beautiful in every way. I am so thankful God allowed you to grow up in our home. Even though it was through devastating circumstances, your loss was certainly my gain. You are a lovely example of what it means to be a Godly woman. It is beautiful to see how God is using you both every week.

Cathy Paliotta and Tina Bruce, I want to thank you both for all of the joy and laughter you have brought to my life over the years. Road life was lonely for me but when I came home, I would always thank God you were there. I hope this book will bless you and keep you on your journey to find MOYD.

Ed and Jeanette Adams, thank you for your generosity and for doing such a wonderful job raising Kevin.

Janice and Bobby Newell, thank you for all of the fun memories at your house in South Georgia! I can't wait to see you again.

Shawn and Janine Hollis, if our daughter turns out even half as wonderful as yours, Kevin and I will be the proudest parents on earth!

Wendy Giorgio, Lynn Guilmette, and Amy Sprunger, thanks for your friendship that has lasted over the decades! Wendy, you have been my biggest cheerleader since the day you forced me to sing at Johnston High Stunt Night—that night changed the trajectory of my life forever!

Gaye Marston and Linda Rainwater, thank you for the wise counsel you have given me over the years.

Lona, thank you for joining me on this journey. You are such an amazing friend and I appreciate everything you do for me on a daily basis. Your heart is like a deep well filled with compassion. The way you love people is a beautiful thing. God has used you mightily in my life and I have no doubt, He has a lot more in store for you.

My three beautiful children, **Santiago, Sebastiano, and Ellianna**—you are the greatest kids in the entire universe and I cannot believe God gave you to ME!!! I am honored to be your mother. To be awarded such incredible treasures on this side of Heaven brings me incredible joy. God has big plans for all three of you!

Lastly, to my husband **Kevin**, you are a faithful man of integrity. You are caring, loving, strong, and mighty! I am so happy God chose you to be my husband. You are the epitome of a Godly man, aka "Martyr Man"—an excellent example to our sons. "Ti amo con tutto il cuore!"

About the Authors

Lona has never been at a loss for words. Whether using spoken, sung, or written words, her goal is always the same—to inspire, bring joy, and restore hope no matter how difficult things may seem.   Lona Renée Fraser is a certified Life Coach, poet, and author of *Habakkuk's Hope*. After her own wrestling conversations with God, He tenderly used Habakkuk's story to fully restore her hope and in turn, Lona helps others unlock their hope as well. She shares her struggles regarding identity, empty nesting, and loss. Lona was also a contributing author alongside Steve Green, Clay Crosse, and Kayla Fioravanti in *360 Degrees of Grief: Reflections of Hope* a Selah Press Anthology filled with stories, poetry, and songs.

She has spent countless hours pouring into the lives of others through one-on-one mentoring. Lona is also the founder of Heartprint Writers' Group equipping, encouraging, and inspiring writers for over a decade. This passionate Italian believes laughter is truly medicine for life. When Cherie, Lona's fellow paisan asked her to co-write *MEET MOYD*, it was a perfect fit! They've had many hilarious writing sessions mixed with some really serious ones. As they wrote, God knit their hearts together as they discussed the fun and heartbreaking aspects of dating. Originally from Upstate NY, Lona now resides in Tennessee with her husband Jim and they have two adult children. She encourages everyone she meets by living out her life's motto—inspire others, inspire yourself.

Connect with Lona:
Website: Livelaughlona.com
Facebook: livelaughlona
Instagram: @live_laugh_lona, @chelonashow

Brendan, Jenney (DIL), Jim, Lona, Tevin (SIL) & Kayla

Some days are like this...

Photo credit: Steven Ploppert

Some days are like that...

Photo credit: Steven Ploppert

Cherie Adams is a recording artist, worship leader, and now author! Formerly of the award-winning Christian music group Avalon, Cherie has garnered numerous awards and accolades including 2 Grammy nominations, 2 Dove Awards, 2 RIAA Gold Certified Albums, and the American Music Award. With over three decades of experience in the music industry, and 10 number-one hits under her belt, her solo debut titled *The Sweet Life* secured her 11th number-one spot on a Christian music inspirational chart with a song she wrote called "Water." Cherie has been featured on major Christian radio stations across the globe and TV appearances on major networks such as TBN, CBN's *The 700 Club*, Macy's Thanksgiving Day Parade, and Canada's longest-running daily television show *100 Huntley Street*.

After suffering through a life-altering event during her dating years that left her completely hopeless about her future, Jesus made Himself tangibly real to her in such a unique way—she has never been the same since. This journey during her single years is what led her to begin writing *MEET MOYD*. She has such a tender heart for single ladies. Cherie's message to the hurting and broken is *"If He can heal me and transform my life, He can do the same for you."*

There is such a need in this world for authenticity and Cherie displays this passionately throughout her writing and music. She recently released a single she wrote and recorded called "Carry Me" presently streaming on all platforms. Her raw emotion and ability to connect intimately with her audience are incomparable. Of all her accomplishments, nothing can compare to being a wife to Kevin and mother to Santiago, Sebastiano, and Ellianna.

Learn more about Cherie at Cherieadams.com
or follow her @cheriepaliottaadams
Facebook.com/cherieadamsofficial

Photo credit: Amy Sprunger   Photo credit: Mike Jordan & Pat Coyne

NEXT STEPS FOR A NEW BELIEVER

Taken from gotquestions.org

1. Make sure you understand salvation.

First John 5:13 tells us, "I write these things to you who believe in the name of the Son of God so that you may know that you have eternal life." God wants us to understand salvation. God wants us to have the confidence of knowing for sure that we are saved. Briefly, let's go over the key points of salvation:

(a) We have all sinned. We have all done things that are displeasing to God (Romans 3:23).

(b) Because of our sin, we deserve to be punished with eternal separation from God (Romans 6:23).

(c) Jesus died on the cross to pay the penalty for our sins (Romans 5:8; 2 Corinthians 5:21). Jesus died in our place, taking the punishment that we deserved. Jesus' resurrection proved that His death was sufficient to pay for our sins.

(d) God grants forgiveness and salvation to all those who place their faith in Jesus—trusting His death as the payment for our sins (John 3:16; Romans 5:1; Romans 8:1).

(e) The Holy Spirit comes to reside permanently within us at the moment of faith. He assures us of everlasting life. He teaches us God's Word and empowers us to live according to it.

That is the message of salvation! If you have placed your faith in Jesus Christ as your Savior, you are saved! All of your sins are forgiven, and God promises to never leave you or forsake you (Romans 8:38–39; Matthew 28:20). Remember, your salvation is secure in Jesus Christ (John 10:28–29). If you are trusting in Jesus alone as your Savior, you can have confidence that you will spend eternity with God in heaven!

2. Find a good church that teaches the Bible.

Don't think of the church as a building. The church is the people. It is very important that believers in Jesus Christ fellowship with one another. That is one of the primary purposes of the church. Now that you have placed your faith in Jesus Christ, we strongly encourage you to find a Bible-believing church in your area and speak to the pastor. Let him know about your new faith in Jesus Christ.

A second purpose of the church is to teach the Bible. You can learn how to apply God's instructions to your life. Understanding the Bible is key to living a successful and powerful Christian life. 2 Timothy 3:16-17 says, "All Scripture is God-breathed and is useful for teaching, rebuking, correcting and training in righteousness, so that the man of God may be thoroughly equipped for every good work."

A third purpose of the church is worship. Worship is thanking God for all He has done! God has saved us. God loves us. God provides for us. God guides and directs us. How could we not thank Him? God is holy, righteous, loving, merciful, and full of grace. Revelation 4:11 declares, "You are worthy, our Lord and God, to receive glory and honor and power, for you created all things, and by your will, they were created and have their being."

3. Set aside time each day to focus on God.

It is very important for us to spend time each day focusing on God. Some people call this a "quiet time." Others call it "devotions," because it is a time when we devote ourselves to God. Some prefer to set aside time in the mornings, while others prefer the evenings. It does not matter what you call this time or when you do it. What matters is that you regularly spend time with God. What events make up our time with God?

(a) Prayer. Prayer is simply talking to God. Talk to God about your concerns and problems. Ask God to give you wisdom and guidance. Ask God to provide for your needs. Tell God how much you love Him and how much you appreciate all He does for you. That is what prayer is all about.

(b) Bible Reading. In addition to being taught the Bible in church, Sunday School, and/or Bible studies – you need to be reading the Bible for yourself. The Bible contains everything you need to know in order to live a successful Christian life. It contains God's guidance for how to make wise decisions, how to know God's will, how to minister to others, and how to grow spiritually. The Bible is God's Word to us. The Bible is essentially God's instruction manual for how to live our lives in a way that is pleasing to Him and satisfying to us.

4. Develop relationships with people who can help you spiritually.

1 Corinthians 15:33 tells us, "Do not be misled: 'Bad company corrupts good character.'" The Bible is full of warnings about the influence "bad" people can have on us. Spending time with

those who engage in sinful activities will cause us to be tempted by those activities. The character of those we are around will "rub off" on us. That is why it is so important to surround ourselves with other people who love the Lord and are committed to Him.

Try to find a friend or two, perhaps from your church, who can help you and encourage you (Hebrews 3:13; 10:24). Ask your friends to keep you accountable in regard to your quiet time, your activities, and your walk with God. Ask if you can do the same for them. This does not mean you have to give up all your friends who do not know the Lord Jesus as their Savior. Continue to be their friend and love them. Simply let them know that Jesus has changed your life and you cannot do all the same things you used to do. Ask God to give you opportunities to share Jesus with your friends.

5. Be baptized.

Many people have a misunderstanding of baptism. The word *baptize* means "to immerse in water." Baptism is the biblical way of publicly proclaiming your new faith in Christ and your commitment to follow Him. The action of being immersed in the water illustrates being buried with Christ. The action of coming out of the water pictures Christ's resurrection. Being baptized is identifying yourself with Jesus' death, burial, and resurrection (Romans 6:3-4).

Baptism is not what saves you. Baptism does not wash away your sins. Baptism is simply a step of obedience, a public proclamation of your faith in Christ alone for salvation. Baptism is important because it is a step of obedience – publicly declaring faith in Christ and your commitment to Him. If you are ready to be baptized, you should speak with a pastor.

Endnotes

Chapter 1:   Thoughts about Yourself

1. Dr. Neil T. Anderson, *Victory Over the Darkness (Gospel Light, 1990),* *https://freedominchrist.com/whoiaminchristbo okmark50pack-saleendsjune30.aspx*
2. Pamela Palmer, "What is the Refiner's Fire," Updated February 2nd, 2024 https://www.biblestudytools.com/bible-study/topical-studies/what-is-the-refiners-fire-in-malachi.html

Chapter 4:   For Such a Time as This

1. "Skin care: 5 tips for healthy skin—Manage Stress" Mayo Clinic website, January 22nd, 2022, https://www.mayoclinic.org/healthy-lifestyle/adult-health/in-depth/skin-care/art-20048237
2. "Skin care: 5 tips for healthy skin—Don't Smoke" Mayo Clinic website, January 22nd, 2022, https://www.mayoclinic.org/healthy-

lifestyle/adult-health/in-depth/skin-care/art-20048237

3. Allie Wergin, "Water: Essential for Your Body," Mayo Clinic website, September 22nd, 2022, https://www.mayoclinichealthsystem.org/hom etown-health/speaking-of-health/water-essential-to-your-body-video

Chapter 6: Social Media & Narcissistic Behavior

1. Simon Kemp, "The time on social media," Global Web Index (GWI), January 31, 2024 https://datareportal.com/reports/digital-2024-deep-dive-the-time-we-spend-on-social-media#:~:text=Research%20from%20GWI%2 0reveals%20that,per%20day%20using%20so cial%20platforms.&text=On%20average%2C %20that%20means%20that,attributed%20to %20social%20media%20platforms.

2. Matthew Keyser, "Reality dating shows promote a toxic view on love," April 27, 2022 https://dailytitan.com/opinion/reality-dating-shows-promote-a-toxic-view-on-

love/article_775e5416-c5ac-11ec-ab8e-
67020ce1d617.html

Chapter 7: The Birds & the Bees

1. "Sexually transmitted infections (STI's)"—
   World Health Organization (WHO),
   https://www.who.int/health-topics/sexually-
   transmitted-infections#tab=tab_

Chapter 9: Red Flags, Rejection & Blind Spots

1. Merriam-Webster, "sovereign (n.)," accessed
   March 4th, 2024 https://www.merriam-
   webster.com/dictionary/sovereign
2. Taryn Hillin, "New Survey Sheds Light On
   What Married Couples Fight About Most,"
   June 3rd, 2014, Updated December 6th, 2017
   https://www.huffpost.com/entry/marriage-
   finances_n_5441012
3. Christy Bieber, J.D., "Revealing Divorce
   Statistics in 2024," Updated January 8th,
   2024
   https://www.forbes.com/advisor/legal/divorce/
   divorce-statistics/

Made in the USA
Columbia, SC
30 May 2024